EXTRAORDINARY PROFITS FROM ORDINARY PROPERTIES

WENDY WHITTAKER-LARGE

EXTRAORDINARY PROFITS FROM ORDINARY PROPERTIES

HOW TO CREATE THE LIFE OF YOUR DREAMS

WITH JUST FIVE PROPERTIES

Copyright
First published by Centre Round Publishers 2019

First edition
ISBN: 9781513607337

DEDICATION

This book is dedicated to my four wonderful boys who are the energy, the inspiration and the purpose behind all I do.
Sam, Jonny, Luke and Tom

TABLE OF CONTENTS

ACKNOWLEDGEMENTS

It would be remiss of me not to mention the people who have helped in so many ways to get this book into print.

Those who inspired me - Robert and Kim Kiyosaki, Rob Moore, Simon Zutshi, Gavin Barry. There are many others whose books I've read, courses I've attended, and speeches I've heard. My fellow speaking community - I love you!

Those who focused me - Daniel Priestley and all at Dent without whom this book probably wouldn't be in existence.

Those who supported me - Mum and Dad, MIL, my wonderful and amazing mentoring clientele and my wider HMO Facebook community.

Those who advised me - and in particular Jackie Moss for her tax advice and accountancy help.

Those who practically helped me, loved me and made endless cups of tea throughout the writing process - Andy (my Darling Husband, editorial assistant and co-motorhome driver). Love you x

And to you, reader, I'm grateful for you too.

Thank you one and all.

INTRODUCTION

A few years ago, I wrote down everything I had learned about setting up and running a small portfolio of Houses of Multiple Occupation (HMOs). Mostly this was to help me document my learning from the whirlwind of activity that had engulfed me since deciding to invest. However, after writing it all down, I realised that I had just about written enough to publish a small book based on my simple system for a 'cookie-cutter' approach to creating high cashflowing properties. That book set out my Five Step System in a quick and easy-to-read format. Since then I have written more about how to start, scale and systemise an HMO business, and I have explored more topics about HMOs in further depth on my blog and social media pages.

I decided last year that I had another book inside me yearning to get out. This book details the reasons why I invest in HMOs in much more detail, and why I believe it is such a successful strategy for investment. You'll learn about how and why I started, the mistakes I made along the way, and what caused my biggest breakthrough.

Most people are raised to get good qualifications, get a job, and swap their time for money for the rest of their lives. They retire on an income that is 50% less than they earned when they had a job, and their lives are constrained until death as a result. Sounds rather depressing, doesn't it? That was the position I found myself in a few years ago. Although I found my job rewarding, I knew there was something missing. The missing piece was freedom. I was always accountable to someone else. You may, like me, have a deep seated drive to create a lifestyle of freedom – where you can choose what you do with the valuable time you have on earth.

Applying the methodology in this book could completely change the trajectory for your own life. If you want to create a new stream of residual income that gives you choices, read on. With the knowledge and confidence you'll gain through reading this book, and by following my system, you could make £1,000 profit per property per month, which could mean that you could be financially free with five properties. The benefit of learning a system is that you can keep repeating it as often as you like until you meet your goal.

Alongside writing, and running a very successful mentoring and training programme, I have continued to develop my property business with an amazing team, which runs the day-to-day operations for me. I have continued to grow our personal portfolio and the portfolio of the investors we work with. I believe in HMOs for the contribution they make to the housing sector and the benefits that good HMOs can make in people's lives. I continue to invest because I believe in the power of HMOs to transform people's lives – both tenants and investors.

Whether or not you decide that HMOs are the right strategy for you, I would still encourage you to take action on your dreams. To believe in your abilities to change your life, no matter what obstacles stand in your way, and to make a decision to change the course of your life takes courage but, more than that, massive action. I am so glad I did – and I know you will be too.

FURTHER HELP AND ADVICE

I lead a lively and interactive Facebook group which I would be delighted if you joined: https://www.facebook.com/groups/TheUltimateHMOSuccessSystem/.

Throughout the book I have offered further templates and spreadsheets, which you can find by going to my publisher's site www.centreround.co.uk. Just click on the 'EPFOP' tab at the top to get all the information you need.

If you are looking to grow, learn and understand more about HMOs and how you can start, scale and systemise your business, please contact me through www.wendywl.uk.

I look forward to hearing from you

Wendy

BACKGROUND AND CONTEXT

CHAPTER 1

HOW I GOT HERE

If you've ever wondered how to create long-term and sustainable income from property without owning a huge portfolio, then I'd be delighted to reveal how, with just a handful of properties, you can create enough cashflow to leave a well-paid job, travel the world and spend more time doing what you love. This book will de-mystify the intrigue that surrounds investing in Houses of Multiple Occupation (HMOs) and show you how you can apply a simple Five-Step System to create the life of your dreams. It's a big claim – and I make no apology for it. Taking a normal house and turning it into a profitable HMO requires many things, including focus, resources and skill.

In this book you'll discover the insider knowledge that I and many more of my clients have applied to create extraordinary profits from ordinary properties, and how we have completely changed our lives as a result. I hope it inspires you to see that you can create a completely new life with just a handful of houses. With just five HMO properties you can create £5,000 income per month. This is a fantastic goal to aim for and will bring you residual income for the rest of your life, along with capital appreciation. For many people that I speak to, this is a life-changing amount of money and replaces their main salary, allowing them to have choices about how they live. If this is you, I would urge you to learn this system, repeat it time and time again, and create the baseline for your future life. It took me many years to realise that the income from a large portfolio of single buy-to-let properties would take me much longer to develop than a handful of HMOs. By doing so, I could replace my salary faster and be freer sooner. My journey started a long time ago, before the phrase 'HMO' was even coined.

I started to dip my toes in the water of multilets, or 'shared housing' as it was then called, in 1996 when I bought my very first investment property. I was hugely excited about the fact that I had a long-term investment for myself and my boys: a pension for me and a legacy for my children. I could officially call myself 'a property investor'. What I didn't realise then was the power that just a handful of well-developed, tenanted properties could do to my income. I began my journey with a simple four-bed ex-council house and it was only years later that I realised how powerful a strategy it was: find an ordinary property and create extraordinary profits by renting the rooms out individually.

I bought the house for £46,000 and, since then, it has over tripled in value. Of course, another benefit to investing in property, which I didn't fully recognise at the time, is capital growth. Renting it out as a single buy-to-let property at the time would have brought in about £400 per month rental income. Once I took off the cost of the finance and insurance, I would have made about £150 per month. By renting it to a group of five students, I made £750 per month. This was as much as I was earning in my insignificant part-time job. It was life-changing, as it meant I could be at home with my children without having to get a full-time job.

After a few years, the college at which the students were studying closed down. I realised the market was changing, so I had to adapt as well. Unceremoniously, I changed this spacious and well-equipped house back into a family home and rented it to a lovely couple. At the time I was sorely disappointed as my income dropped dramatically. Renting the house to five students had made me much more money than letting it to a family, so I was forced to increase my hours at work. I kept the house but constantly wondered if I would ever make any money in property. In those days there was very little property training or education available, and I was naive and ignorant about the various property money-making strategies. I procrastinated interminably about other deals due to my lack of confidence.

My progress was not just slow – it was imperceptible. I had no-one to go to or ask for advice, so I muddled along, making mistakes and occasionally just getting lucky with good tenants. I really had no idea what I was doing. My story was one of fear and indecision until I turned the corner after an epiphany moment years later.

Over the next few years I remortgaged that house and bought a few more buy-to-lets (a couple were bought at auction). In 1998 I had another baby and, when he was old enough, I started to focus on my career. My property portfolio was very much a part-time hobby. I treated it like a hobby – and it paid me as much. I got divorced, remarried and had yet another son. By this time, four boys was quite enough – I was clearly good at reproduction, but I now wanted to reproduce income, not another mouth to feed! Family life was busy, but also stressful.

Then in 2001, there was a shock to my life when my two eldest boys were diagnosed with a rare form of Cystic Fibrosis. This is a genetically inherited disease for which there is no cure, affecting primarily the lungs and other internal organs. Suddenly our lives were thrown into turmoil with daily physiotherapy, antibiotics and regular hospital visits. It was immensely time consuming, energy sapping and emotionally draining. The boys' health was always on my mind, and yet I was aware of my other sons' needs, and my wish to create a balanced family life. I always had an eye on the future, and perhaps this was what drove me more than anything else.

Although I had a good job (I was a lecturer at a local university), I wasn't happy. I was unfulfilled and felt as if I had no freedom – always being answerable to someone else. My job took up a lot of my thinking time as well as my actual time and I found I had little energy left after dealing with the boys and their increasing needs.

The financial crash of 2008 came and went and we were in a new world. Work was all-consuming and time whizzed by. It was much later, in 2012, before I realised what I had been missing on the property front. By this time, lots had changed: legislation, building regulations, tenants' expectations, the internet. I felt that everything I'd learned first time round no longer counted; it wasn't applicable any more.

The day everything changed for me was in early April 2012. I had been feeling completely lost. Despite having a small portfolio of buy-to-let properties, I lacked desire to do more.

Perhaps because I felt inadequate, I had a corresponding paucity of direction, focus and clarity. I sensed that my life was meant for more than swapping my time for money. But I had no idea how to change it. Although the role at the university was well paid, flexible and meaningful, there was a nagging feeling of emptiness. I was searching for more – but I didn't know what that more was. I felt guilty for these feelings. I had a warm and loving marriage, four amazing children, a lovely home and regular holidays. I had a local job that was reasonably flexible and regular income. The boys' health was a constant concern, but I reasoned that I was not the one with the greatest cross to bear. When all was still and quiet, there was a nagging ache in my soul. It was the ache of a call – a call to have more and to be more. And it started with the call to do more.

One Friday evening, I came home from work and dropped my bags on the hall floor. The boys were already home from school and my husband, Andy, had collected our youngest son from nursery. Chaos abounded – quite usual for a Friday night. I flicked through the pile of letters waiting for me and noticed a purple postcard lying on top of the pile. It was an invitation to a property investment seminar. I was intrigued. The postcard mentioned the name of a property expert and this prompted me immediately to order his book on Kindle. I hadn't heard of Robert Kiyosaki before, and I wasn't going to commit to a seminar with a so-called expert unless I had first checked out who he really was. As I read his book *'Rich Dad, Poor Dad*, I felt my chest starting to expand. Heat permeated through my body as I devoured his words. I voraciously gobbled up the story, the models and the theory that underpinned his approach. He spoke about income-producing assets, and how your house is a liability. All of it struck a deep chord with me. I sensed that this was right – and was what I had been looking for. His method, his actions and his knowledge created absolute clarity in my mind. It was an epiphany. I suddenly realised what I had been missing. There was an opportunity waiting for me – I just had to grab it and run with it. As I finished the book, I realised that I had been wasting so much time. I had let my sense of 'lack' – what I didn't have – stop me from getting what I wanted – which was freedom. My choice to swap my time for money was antithesis to what I really desired. And yet I had eschewed the path that could have offered me that chance only a few years before. My procrastination had truly messed up what were probably some of the best years ever for investing in property. I felt like I had missed the boat – and boy was I sore about that!

I knew that my fear and lack of confidence had held me back from expansion first time round. So now I knew it was time to throw myself in. I was being given a second chance – and despite still having no idea what I was doing, my mind was made up. The opportunity was there – all I had to do was say yes. I was determined to revisit what I already knew – that making income from taking a run-of-the-mill house, and letting the rooms by creating a House of Multiple Occupation (the new legal term for multilets) could change my life. I wasn't going to let this opportunity pass me by. The motivation and focus welled up within me like a gushing geyser – ready to explode. My mind raced with possibilities and energy. I jumped onto the PC and spent hours learning all I could about Houses of Multiple Occupation (HMOs) and searching for the right house. I moved from a crossroads to a motorway, and felt an internal surge of acceleration. I was as nervous as I was elated and determined. My aim was clear: to build a legacy and a lifestyle through generating extraordinary profits from ordinary properties.

Perhaps you can relate to feeling stuck, or slow, or scared. It's a feeling that gnaws away at you, until you realise that other people have broken free and that it's time for you to do just that. This could be your crossroads moment – and I hope you choose to leave the rat-race and join the property entrepreneurial revolution, where you can live life on your own terms.

Since that day in 2012 my life completely changed. I went from being a stressed-out mother of four, with a part-time job *and* a part-time business, to having time and freedom to do what I wanted. I built a multi-million pound property portfolio using other people's money – and I now do many other things aside from property investing. In 2014 (just two years after starting over) I resigned from my job and the following year, once we had enough income from property to cover our wage income, my husband Andy left his job. We now have over 140 rooms, which we own or manage, and we've also been able to expand the business through ownership of commercial property. We have a lettings agency that specialises in HMOs and we employ a small team to manage the rooms. Through systemisation of the business, we can do other things with our time, so we have more freedom than ever. There is no point running a business if you still have to swap your time for money.

Andy and I enjoy running, triathlons and keeping fit, and I also have a training and mentoring business through which I help others create portfolios that give them cash and time freedom. It's been a great delight to me to support my boys on their own investing and entrepreneurial journey too. I am the chair of our local YMCA and I ran the London Marathon this year. I have travelled the world and, last year alone, we had nine weeks away as a family. I'm also profoundly grateful for the health of my boys, which, despite their conditions, has not drastically deteriorated in the way that it might have. We are involved in our local community and continue to learn, grow and educate ourselves. I don't say this to brag – just to illustrate how much investing in property can and will change your life, if you make a decision to say 'yes'.

You might be right at the beginning of your investment journey and looking for a way out of your job. You might already have some experience in property and are now looking to expand. Perhaps you have run out of your own money to invest. You may be worried about providing for your pension or have a desire to leave a legacy for your family. Whatever is your history or background, you can change your future. Don't be like me and waste the opportunity of a lifetime. Learn all you can from reading this book and applying the lessons. It's absolutely true that, with a handful of HMOs, you can create continual cashflow for you and your family – enough for you to leave your job, travel and spend time with your loved ones. This book is here to help you do just that. But before I get stuck into the nuts and bolts of HMOs, and how you can address *all* these issues through investing, I'd like to share my story with you in more detail.

CHAPTER 2

ORDINARY PROPERTY: EXTRAORDINARY PROFITS

If you are just getting started, and wonder how you too can create life-changing income, I thought it would be worth letting you in on my story. Although it was over 20 years ago when I started out, the themes within my story are the same themes you may be facing today: ignorance and education; risk and reward; trial and error; fear and excitement.

Due to lack of direction, and other priorities, my portfolio grew very slowly between 1996 - when my story started - and 2012. You could say I took a pregnant pause. I now realise that I lost momentum due to lack of clarity. I don't want that to happen to you. I want you to find the motivation and support to change your life – whatever position you find yourself in today. I don't believe you would be reading this book if you didn't have a deeper reason for choosing it. I hope that by sharing my story you'll see how you can do this too and how, by following my simple Five-Step System, you'll learn exactly how to make it happen. It won't take many properties to change your life, if you follow the system. Just a handful could radically change your life forever.

Let me take you back to the beginning. 1996 was a time when money for us was *very* tight. My then husband was a teacher and we had two young children to support. So I was working part-time for a few hours a week just to bring in some extra income. We owned an old red Peugeot 405 estate and, every time it had a service, it seemed that there was always one more problem.

It was a bright, warm day in May as I drove home from my part-time job, looking forward to seeing the boys' faces when I collected them from school. Usually I would pull up and jump out, round them up and bundle them into the car, before making our way home. I was driving along the main road through our village, about to slow down to turn left. As I did so, I put my foot on the brake, only to find it wasn't working. No matter how hard I pressed the foot pedal, it would not slow the car down.

I began to panic as I approached the junction where I needed to turn in left. I pumped the footbrake hard, and pressed on the clutch to move into first gear just to get some control. At least then I could swerve into the side of the pavement if I couldn't stop. I gripped the handbrake. I was beginning to sweat as I saw the junction ahead and I still couldn't stop the car. I wasn't travelling fast, but even 20 miles an hour when you can't stop feels like 60mph. There was only one thing for it – a handbrake stop. I yanked the handbrake, both feet pushing hard and firmly on the brake and clutch pedals simultaneously, turning the steering wheel hard to the left, and with a loud screech, managed to pull the car into the side road, just as a car turned out of the junction almost into my path on the main road. The driver glanced my way with a look of sudden shock, as if realising we had had a very near miss.

I felt exhausted. I had only travelled a few metres, but it was one of the most petrifying moments of my whole life. Why were the brakes suddenly not working? What would have happened if I couldn't stop the car? What terrible accident might have happened?

I got out, shaking, and took a few deep breaths. We only lived around the corner, so I got back in the driver's seat and slowly drove the car home. As I pulled up on the drive I deliberately utilised my new handbrake skills to pull the car to a halt. I walked round to collect the boys from school, trying not to look shaken, not mentioning to them mummy's scary moment.

This car was obviously not safe to drive, and I had to take action immediately to repair it as it was literally a car crash waiting to happen. Within a few days it was at the garage – was that the third time this month? The bill to get it fixed was a price we could barely afford, yet the brakes had to be repaired or we would be facing life without a car, which was untenable at that point in our lives. I paid the bill, reluctantly knowing there was no money left in the savings account – yet again – and wondered when life would start to be easier financially.

It was against this backdrop that we had a call a few days later to say that my husband's grandma had died. It was sad to say goodbye to a dearly loved woman and even more touching when we discovered that she had built her own legacy, not just for her children, but for her grandchildren.

A small pot of money in the form of shares was going to be coming our way. At that point we were faced with a decision that had never presented to us before – how to spend it. We debated what to do with the money. Should we buy a new car, go on holiday or carry out some upgrades to our own home? We had a long list of necessities and luxuries that we could buy, but I knew that unless we invested wisely, the money would run out faster than a packet of jaffa cakes in the hands of a toddler.

You too might get a lucky break like we did. This little pot of seed-funding started my property journey and, without it, I would never look back. You might not have a stash of cash to get started though, so what can you do? There are many options available if you don't yet have enough money to get started (some are covered in 'Fund It'). Learn all you can about how money and property works. Look after your money wisely and have belief that you will find that money. I've seen more times than I can count that when someone desires something with all their heart and is committed to making it happen, amazing things happen.

We decided then and there to take a leap of faith and invest in our very first property aside from our family home. I had little knowledge and even less education about this lucrative and fascinating opportunity. It was my mum who had encouraged me to think about investing, and she had roped me into subscribing to a publication called *Property Auction News*. Each month I read about the amazing properties being bought and sold at auction, and how much money was being made by those brave enough to try this method of purchase. I read it with interest, but had no idea how to go about the process of refurbishment or financing. What really piqued my interest was the income that I could create from property investing, in a compellingly passive way. Alongside my few pounds per week working as a learning assistant in a school, I figured that this could be just the answer to allowing me to be at home but also have an additional source of cashflow.

I was chatting to a friend one day outside the school gates and casually mentioned my idea. Unlike other people who had reacted with surprise, caution or sheer ignorance about property investing, she told me that her husband had been buying up property in the local area for the last few years and renting it to students as shared accommodation. I was intrigued. Our town had a small college campus on it, linked to another one a few miles away. It was not the main hub of academic activity but ran specialist courses such as Creative Arts, Sports Science and Design and Technology degrees. In fact, it was how I had ended up living here: a few years before I had studied my first degree in Creative Arts. I hadn't realised that there was a need locally for accommodation, having lived on campus myself and then moved across town during my degree. The thought of being poacher turned gamekeeper fascinated me, as I realised I had seen it from the other side of the fence, as a student myself.

My friend invited me over to her house to talk to them both and, that evening, I learned all about how they got started, what kind of profits they were making and how they were providing good quality accommodation for students. This was before Buy-to-let mortgages had been created, so the only way to get funding from banks was via a business loan. And the only way to get a business loan was to write a business plan. So that was my next move.

Writing a business plan for one property was not exactly rocket science. I just had to describe a bit about myself, a bit about the property I wanted to buy, how I would make money doing it and what I needed from the bank. It wasn't especially daunting, but halfway through I realised that one side of A4 would not impress the business manager of the TSB, with whom I had an appointment the following week for a finance meeting.

So I decided to carry out some research about my chosen market, and the local vicinity where I was intending to invest and, more importantly perhaps, why the TSB should lend me the money I needed. As part of my market research, the only place I knew where to start was the library (this was 1996 remember). As soon as I entered our local library, I saw the library assistant who at the time was piling up books on the desk. I approached her and asked where I could go to research local property market trends, especially student housing. She pointed a long thin finger across the library to the opposite wall, labelled 'Gardening and Practical DIY'...

'Um, I'm not looking for how to build a house, just information on demand and local population information' I hinted.

'Yes, and I'm pointing to the place which I think could help you most. I'm not pointing at the DIY and Gardening books. I'm pointing through the window next to them – can you see Bridgfords Estate Agency?'

'Oh yes ... Of course, thank you' I humbly said (wondering why I didn't think of that as I exited into the bright sunlight and made my way across the road).

One of my good friends, Chris, had up until recently been branch manager at this local estate agents and I had occasionally popped in to see how he was. Although he was no longer working here, Diane, one of the negotiators, was sitting at the front desk and immediately recognised me when I walked in.

'Diane, I wonder if you can help me', I said.

'Sure, what are you looking for, Wendy? Something larger for your growing brood perhaps?'

'Actually, we've come into a bit of money and I'm thinking about buying an investment property. I'm here to ask you about the demand for student housing and whether you think this is a good place to buy something to rent out.'

'Well, Wendy, of course I'd be happy to tell you what I know. Just come here as there's something I really have to show you …'. And, with that, she took my hand and led me across the room to see the details of a new house they had just taken on to sell. 'This property is ideal for you, Wendy. There are five students already living there who are only in their second year. They want to stay, so you won't even need to get new tenants. It's got plenty of space, four bedrooms, two bathrooms and a large kitchen diner. When are you free to come for a viewing?'

Early the next afternoon, I was nervously standing outside the house on Moorhouse Avenue trying to look as if I knew what I was doing. The property looked a good size, on a corner plot and with a large front and back garden. You could tell it was students who lived there – all the curtains were pulled closed, the lawn was overgrown and as I walked up the path I had to dodge the weeds. The house had an internal garage, which the students had used to store their sporting equipment as most of them living there were Sports Science students. They were fit and healthy – but looking around inside they didn't apply their strength to the washing up. Or the mowing of the lawn in the front or back gardens.

However, I could see beyond that, having been a student myself not too long before. And now with two boys I was fairly comfortable and very familiar with mess. The fact that the current tenants wanted to stay was a real bonus and, listening to Diane tell me about current demand convinced me that I would not have a problem letting the house after this cohort had left. Their rents were a good amount, they were happy to share the bills and organise them as they had been doing. The last thing they wanted was for a new landlord to come and change anything. That suited me fine. All I planned on doing was giving them my bank details so they could pay the rent and having a quick mow of the lawn. I could see this was a match made in heaven.

I left the viewing feeling that wonderful mixture of nervousness and excitement. The feeling you get when you know you are on the cusp of doing something out of your comfort zone, something that will stretch and test you, but that also has the potential to be life-changing. *That* feeling. As I arrived home and shared my growing excitement with the family, I knew that I had found the property that would launch my new business. There was still the matter of the business plan that had to be written. But now I had a project with which to create real profit and loss projections and show evidence of rental received and costs incurred. A couple of late nights' work ensued, after which

I had my business plan ready and complete.

The following week, I met with the brand new 'lending manager' at TSB in Hanley, Stoke-on-Trent, nervously clutching my neatly word-processed four-page business plan. I was shown into a lovely bright office – and it was there that I was first introduced to the wonderful world of bank lending. At this point in time, buy-to-let mortgages were just a bank manager's dream and borrowing needed to be authorised in person and with approval from a local branch. Tentatively, I presented my business plan to the lending manager, who skimmed through it and placed it neatly and decisively on the table.

'What makes you think this is a business, Mrs Whittaker', he asked forcibly.

'Well, I hope to grow it in time. If this one works, then I could do more and more', I answered.

'Ah, so you're not necessarily going to stop at one student house then?'

'Um, no, well, yes I'd like to buy more but well, ahem, I'll have to see how this one goes first I suppose', I answered falteringly. I couldn't at that point conceive of having more than one property to rent out. The risk of this first one was testing my nerve as it was.

It seemed to be enough as, within a few minutes, he asked me to sign a couple of documents. 'We will need you to open a TSB account, Mrs Whittaker. The money will be in your bank account within five working days', he stated decisively.

'Oh, ok, wow, ha. Thank you ...', I said, as I jumped up and shook his hand, beaming from ear to ear.

My HMO journey had begun. In just four weeks the conveyancing was completed and I was back at Bridgfords, collecting my keys. Within a few weeks it was the start of the new academic year, and I was busy arranging the move-back-in of the previous tenants who had been away for the summer. New tenancies were signed with the students, in line with the assured shorthold tenancy legislation that had just come into force, and I was up and away. I had done very little to the house since getting the keys. After all, the tenants were the same people. The empty wine bottles lined up on the kitchen window sill were theirs, as was the pile of rotting washing up in the sink. I decided not to rock the boat too much. So, when they came back in September, it was exactly how they had left it. I bought a receipt book and, as each tenant rolled up with a car full of bedding and personal items, I was there, ready to collect their rent and deposit.

I've now been investing in property ever since, much of it at a snail's pace, and I have made many errors and faced cul-de-sacs along the way. I did it whilst raising a family and working, which brought me many distractions and responsibilities. It was only when I got well and truly stuck in a dead-end job a few years later that I realised I'd been focusing my energy in the wrong direction. I came to understand that, for a few short years, if I let go of my fears, my ignorance, my doubts and pressed on to invest in property in a really *big* way, I could create a lifestyle – not just a legacy. I was sitting on top of an opportunity to create a business that would bring me not only great income but also freedom.

An exercise that will focus your energies like nothing else is writing down your financial freedom figure. Having clarity about what that amount is per month will drive you forward whenever you face obstacles and challenges. I would recommend right now that you take a pen and paper and write down the amount you need per month in order to leave your job and create a new life. Keep it somewhere you can see it each day. Then, every month, assess your residual income (from property and other assets). Gradually you'll see your residual income growing. It will also help focus your time and resources on growing your assets, rather than your liabilities.

We can dream about the future, we can eulogise about the past, but where are we in the present? Let's now look at how we got here.

CHAPTER 3

THE HISTORY OF HMOs

'Study the past if you would define the future'
—Confucius

Looking back through the history of the private rented sector (PRS), it becomes obvious that what we now call Houses of Multiple Occupation (HMOs), have been a mainstay in the rental housing sector for many years. Even before they were officially recognised as HMOs in the Housing Act 1985, which first defined an HMO as 'a house which is occupied by persons who do not form a single household', people have chosen to live in rented accommodation where there were shared facilities. Today we may refer to them as 'multilets', or shared houses but, in essence, any property that is shared by three or more people who form separate households (i.e. they are not related or in a relationship) is by definition an HMO.

HMOs are a product of a wider society and, to this day, the debates surrounding their development and use continue to have political, social and ethical overtones. Within the whole subject of housing, HMOs are but a small part, yet over the last 10 years they have moved to be increasingly under the spotlight. Local councils, national government and civic communities all want to have their say on the rules and regulations by which HMOs should be run and managed. Some of these make sense within a health and safety discourse – there can be little argument about the need to keep tenants safe and protected from the hazards that shared housing can generate. However, there is a much more deeply embedded purpose to the changes brought about by the government, which is to rid the housing sector of private landlords and make HMOs a much more complex property investment strategy. This ideology is mirrored in the government's approach, which appears to want to strangle the private sector in favour of state-led housing provision – whether that be build to rent, help to buy or any other three-word phrase that is another excuse for quantitative easing and state control.

Many of those shouting the loudest against the PRS have never stepped inside an HMO and have no notion of the current changes and types of rooms and provision made for tenants. They are reliant on outdated images of dirty, dilapidated and damp housing, as epitomised in the 1980s comedy *The Young Ones*. Modern HMOs in reality are as far from this as is possible to imagine, and it is the determination and desire of many private landlords to fight tooth and nail against this image, by creating warm, hospitable, contemporary and exciting spaces in which to live. I hope to demonstrate through an examination of the history and types of accommodation of this sort (boarding houses, hostels, dormitories and variously named comparisons) that the flexibility, provision and ultimately service provided by HMOs in the private sector is vital to our economy and housing provision. If you are considering investing in HMOs, I believe that it is in the power of the local landlord and investor to challenge drastically the notion that HMOs are unclean, unsuitable and unattractive places to live. I also believe that, in offering shared accommodation, you are providing a hugely valuable place to live for many people who, for various reasons, find other types of accommodation unsuited to their needs. HMOs are a cornerstone of local housing provision and absolutely central to the tenant market in many areas of the country. While we might idealise the notion that 'An Englishman's home is his castle' (notwithstanding the sexist and racist implications of such a phrase!), I wonder if, in today's society, this still holds true. Changing lifestyles, freedom of movement and, ironically, the financial choices that such living allows are just some of the benefits that tenants receive from living in these properties.

THE VICTORIAN PAST

Since the Victorian era, those who could not afford to buy their own house had two options when it came to renting: choose between social housing or private rental. In fact, according to my research, until the beginning of the twentieth century, 90% of all houses were rented from private landlords. Many of these landlords were landowners who owned a significant portfolio of properties. They were also employers and large business owners. But given the population explosion across the UK during this period and the pressing need for accommodation in towns and cities, their properties were often slum-like, damp and cold. Little housing regulation existed, so cheap accommodation often meant putting up with lack of sanitation, unsafe living conditions and, consequently, vermin (and that's not just a barbed reference to the other human inhabitants!).

Government began to pass various Acts mainly aimed at addressing the worst areas of housing unfit for habitation or to improve or demolish existing houses. The most important Act came in 1885: the Housing for the Working Classes Act.[1] Efforts were made to build and regulate private common lodging houses that catered for those in the most need. They provided accommodation, mostly for single men in dormitories, many providing basic beds for some of the poorest people in society. They were mostly run by charitable trusts or voluntary organisations. However, in almost all areas, efforts to clear slum areas exceeded all new house construction, effectively reducing the total number of low-cost housing available. Most pre-1919 corporation housing was built cheaply, taking the form of high-density tenement blocks of flats with small rooms and limited facilities, including shared kitchen and toilets and no running hot water. Typically, rents were high, which was no comfort to those on low and irregular wages, and this kind of housing therefore was not available for the very poor. It wasn't until after the First World War that housing became a real priority.

After the First World War, the government passed the Housing, Town Planning &c. Act of 1919,[2]which compelled local authorities to build council houses. Along with this new alternative to private renting, rent controls and security of tenure (which had been introduced during the war) made being a private landlord much less attractive. The number of people renting privately began to shrink, and the number renting socially began to grow. By 1939, the percentage of people renting socially was around 58% compared to 10% renting privately, with the

1 http://www.legislation.gov.uk/ukpga/Vict/48-49/72.
2 http://www.legislation.gov.uk/ukpga/1919/35/enacted.

remainder owning their own homes. The effects of the Second World War led to a huge increase in house building. This, coupled with novel access to loans and mortgages, enabled many ordinary people to buy their own home for the first time. Suburbia boomed.

In terms of shared housing in London and in other cities, bedsits and shared accommodation became more prevalent. Access to public transport allowed people to travel further afield and to work away from home. Immigration brought people to the UK who could not buy their own home and had little cash for rent. So the need for inexpensive shared housing grew steadily.

THE 1970s ONWARD

By 1971, the number of people renting socially and privately was almost at equivalent levels, and the number of people renting and owning was equal. This was the first time in UK history that as many people owned property as rented it. This was a time during which people were encouraged to 'settle down' by buying their own house. Underpinned by the era of modern government that ushered in an ideology of the rights of the individual to own their own home, many families took advantage of an opportunity not afforded to their parents.

Later, in the 1980s, under her Conservative government, Prime Minister Margaret Thatcher introduced 'right to buy' – a scheme to allow council tenants to buy their house. This took off and, paired with a continuing deregulation of the banking sector, allowed council tenants to buy their homes at a discount and 'realise the dream of owning capital – something that could be passed onto their children. Property ownership soared – some 1 million council homes had been sold by 1987 and home-ownership had increased to around 63%, very near its historic peak.'[3].

1988 saw the introduction of the assured shorthold tenancy and the removal of rent controls. This reduced restrictions for private landlords, yet also gave protection to tenants' rights: 'Being a landlord was a viable business once again – it had hit its nadir, and was now climbing upwards.'[4] Throughout each of these decades in the twentieth century, the use of properties to house individuals either on a room-by-room or bedsit basis had been growing. Working patterns were changing and the need for flexible, yet affordable, accommodation was growing. Alongside this, the student population also needed more accommodation. So throughout the 1990s there was a steady growth of 'shared houses', 'multilet accommodation' or what was later defined by the Housing Act 2004 as a House of Multiple Occupation.

HOUSING ACT 2004

The Housing Act 2004 was a significant piece of legislation, which established a more complex definition of an HMO with regard to the relationship of the tenants to one another, the responsibilities of the landlord or manager, and the standard of facilities in the property. The Act also introduced the requirement for certain HMOs to be subject to mandatory licensing. Licensing was restricted to large HMOs, which were

3 Commercial Trust, 2013.
4 Ibid.

defined in the Act as properties with five or more tenants forming more than one household, sharing facilities such as kitchen and bathroom and/or toilets over three or more floors. There was no reference to the number of bedrooms. On 1 October 2018 the Licensing of Houses in Multiple Occupation Order 2018 amended the large HMO definition in the 2004 Act by abolishing the 'threeor more floors' requirement for licensing and, in addition, introduced rules for minimum room sizing (rooms for couples have to be at least $10m^2$, and single or individual rooms $6.52m^2$).

Prior to the Housing Act 2004, many properties were being used as shared houses, multilets and other variously named configurations. The idea was, in essence, the same across the board. Dividing a house into rooms that could be used as bedrooms – each separately rentable, with shared communal living spaces such as kitchens and bathrooms – proved to be an economic use of space and also created affordable accommodation for many tenants. For landlords and investors who saw the opportunities and embraced the challenges of owning HMOs, this proved in many cases to be a shrewd investment. Even withstanding the additional running costs, including the burden of full responsibility for maintenance (and the inevitable increase caused by housing multiple tenants at once) the profits achieved were as much as five times that of a single buy-to-let property. Depending on the arrangement and the tenant type, tenants were responsible for splitting all costs such as utility bills among themselves. Typically, this was most common in the student sector, where students committed to living in a property together as a group for at least a year. (They often hold 'joint and several liability' contracts, meaning that each is individually and jointly responsible for making the rent payments.)

There were challenges though. Before 1996 and the passing of the Landlord and Tenant Act, 'buy-to-let' mortgages had not yet been created. Lending was in the form of commercial mortgages or loans as many lenders considered these properties to be commercial enterprises and so did not offer mortgage products to finance the purchase or refurbishment costs.

It was at this time that I bought my first property and had to make an application for a bank loan to fund the purchase. My student multilet fitted the bill perfectly, with five lettable rooms, a large kitchen diner and two bathrooms. In common with other college and university towns I saw a continual and growing demand in our local area for shared accommodation, as student numbers steadily grew. Alongside this, in cities and larger conurbations across the country, shared HMO-type accommodation was also on the increase. Mainly limited to those with low incomes, claiming benefits, or limited resources, shared houses became far more prolific in the 1990s and 2000s, after the loosening of legislation on banks that allowed the creation of loans for rental property and the birth of the buy-to-let market. Initially, lenders were reluctant and unprepared for the HMO market, tending to lump HMO investments in with general buy-to-let lending. However, it was quickly recognised that 'shared houses', or 'multilets' as they were more commonly known, needed a specialist form of lending.

THE MORTGAGE MARKET FOR HMOs

Just as this additional mortgage product market was emerging, and it seemed that anyone who was even slightly financially educated had a buy-to-let property, the financial crisis of 2007/8 hit and, suddenly, banks and building societies clamped down on lending. As a result, there was a tangible tightening of lending requirements, making it much harder for retail buyers (residential buyers) to get a mortgage. Banks became more cautious about who they would lend to, as well as the levels at which they would lend. Those who were already in buy-to-let had the benefit of experience and a track record upon which to call when applying for new borrowing. They had the advantage of being in a market where there were rising numbers of people needing to rent and a growth in immigration.

Lenders often had commercial arms that had previously focused on pure commercial property, multiple lending or large investors. Security was raised against the property, but the loans were not regulated and were treated as business loans with access to further drawdowns when certain criteria were met. These departments were now becoming more involved in mortgage lending on HMOs. As regulation was introduced that demonstrated that traditional buy-to-let was not suited to HMO lending, mortgage companies started to create specific commercial HMO products, which closed the gap between commercial and residential lending.

THE STUDENT SECTOR

In parallel to the wider rental market across this decade, a further area of HMO growth was in the student sector. In 1950, 17,300 students were awarded their initial degrees and 2,400 were awarded higher degrees at UK universities, against a UK population of 50 million people. The vast majority of these students lived on campus in university student accommodation or they found lodgings locally. Over the next three decades, political and social pressure changed higher education from the elitist system of access to academic scholarship to a more universal system. This led to a steady growth in student numbers, with 30% of school leavers accessing higher education across the 1970s, '80s and '90s. Accommodation provision always lags behind population movement. So, just as the UK government was debating funding for higher education and the merging of higher education institutions from colleges and polytechnics into full university-style institutions, student numbers were rapidly growing. Investors saw the demand and reacted appropriately, adapting and kitting out properties for shared student accommodation.

Letting agents did not generally cater to the market (except in the case of student HMOs where universities and colleges had their own listings that landlords could use to advertise available properties). Over time, particularly in university towns and cities, specialist student shared housing letting agents appeared, which enabled investors to create passive income without the day-to-day work of managing the property. This encouraged further investment. The higher education market in the UK is undeniably competitive and, over time, universities realised that to attract the best students, with the deepest pockets, accommodation had to be of an equally high standard to that of the onsite facilities offered. Until the early 1990s, on university open days, if the accommodation officer could only suggest to prospective students and their parents that the choice of accommodation was limited to campus rooms (which often felt like you were in a hi-de-hi holiday camp!) or off-site grungy shared housing, you had to accept that this was student life, and part of the 'experience' of living away from home. As student fees were introduced in the late 1990s, and increased markedly to address the changing nature of funding in the higher education sector, universities came to the conclusion that they had to create accommodation that would meet the rising expectations of their new intakes. No longer was it appropriate for the accommodation officer to draw up a list of available accommodation, having liaised with the individual landlord, and print it on a rather insipid-looking piece of buff paper.

By the early 2000s, the new breed of students (who were by now contributing financially to their higher education in the form of student loans) started to require better facilities both on campus and in their new 'home from home'. Dirty, shoddy, badly maintained accommodation was no longer acceptable as part of university culture. And universities had funding made available to them from central government to allow them to build purpose-built accommodation. These were accommodation blocks that had the latest technology in-built, such as CAT5 data points, power sockets enough for any female boudoir, and superfast broadband. Rooms were all en-suite, saving the hassle and embarrassment of sharing, and contained enough space for a desk, wardrobe and chest of drawers. Communal lounges with flatscreen TVs and DVD players were provided – not just for 50 students at once, but for small 'pods' – five to ten students at a time. Kitchens were well equipped, with plenty of storage space and cooking equipment, and the accommodation was warm, damp-free and was all-inclusive (sometimes full board) so there were no unexpected bills or debates about who was using the most gas. The large influx of extra funding for accommodation meant that universities could provide students with the choice of living on campus for the full three years of their university degree.

Over the last decade, student numbers have continued to rise and the proportion of English 18-year-olds applying for a university place is now at its highest on record, at 37.8%, equating to 230,320 applications. Since the changes in tuition fee arrangements in 2012/13, there has been an upward trend in the number of first-year students taking first degrees. Despite the increase in fees, and the student loan system, student numbers across the UK are continuing to rise at a rate of 2–3% per annum. Overseas applicants and part-time and mature students are part of the continuing uptake. However, the numbers of 18-year-olds in the population is in decline and this is having an impact on the actual numbers of students now attending university. According to Cushman and Wakefield (2015),[5] bed spaces in the private sector grew by 28% from 2013 to 2015. There has been significant development of studio-type rooms, increasing by 41% in just one year (2014–2015). Room numbers are likely to continue to increase due to the large pipeline of private sector planning applications and approvals across the sector, as well as significant plans by universities to invest in their accommodation portfolios. The development of purpose-built student accommodation (PBSA) is proving a lucrative sell to institutional investors and, with its well-funded institutional pool, has created a new threat for small investors and landlords in the student market.

5 Cushman and Wakefield, 2015.

THE PRESENT DAY

Fast-forward to the present day and we can see how, despite changes in the wider housing sector, the impact of issues such as Brexit, the context of the wider economy and fluctuations in policy and rental markets, and student funding, HMOs still accommodate hundreds of thousands of people across the UK. It continues to be a vital and vibrant market.

This brief history of the steady acceptance of shared housing into our society and the valuable accommodation that it provides is part of my argument for continued support, input and evolution of HMOs. There is a new trend emerging – that of 'co-living', which seeks to eliminate some of the separate and sometimes lonely existence that tenants can experience in HMOs. Co-living instead seeks to embed a culture of community and shared experiences. These are future trends worth staying abreast of. These are exciting times for HMOs. The financial landscape is changing too, with many more products available for limited company borrowing. It is becoming a go-to strategy for many relatively inexperienced investors to create fast cashflow.

Nowadays, you don't need money and you don't need to be an expert in the building trade to make this strategy work. HMOs are not a secret strategy, but they are more advanced than simple buy-to-lets. Being well-educated and having sound advice will enable you to do what many hundreds have already done and continue to do before you – take an ordinary property and use it to make extraordinary profits.

CHAPTER 4

WHERE WE ARE NOW

'An investment in knowledge pays the best interest'
—Benjamin Franklin

To understand an investment, you need to understand its context, creation and claim. HMOs are no exception. Understanding the current market is core to your ability to spot trends, see opportunities and develop a portfolio that will bring you returns for life. When I began phase 2 of my investing journey in 2012, I knew that my knowledge was insufficient for the task at hand. So, I studied, went on courses and learned as much as I could from those who had gone before me – by standing on the shoulders of giants you could say. In Part 2 I'll share all my practical tools and my Five-Step System that I developed for creating a high cashflowing HMO portfolio. However, this current section is just as important. Understanding the environment in which you are investing is critical to being an educated and effective investor. Spotting trends, knowing the needs of the market and being informed about the economy are just as important as knowing how to get a FENSA certificate for your new windows.

You will know which areas will work and which will not. And you'll have insight and spot opportunities that others cannot see.

HMO LICENSING

Since 2004, any HMO (including student shared housing) has been subject to requiring a mandatory licence from the local authority if it was over three storeys and had more than five rooms. The local authority was required to hold a database of licensed HMOs and was required to inspect them annually. These properties were subject to higher safety standards and more rigorous management than other HMOs.

Since October 2018, all HMOs with more than five rooms are licensable. With councils seeing reductions to budgets and staffing, and pressures linked to the economy, public sector pension provision, and public sector working conditions, more staff are being rapidly recruited across the UK to deliver on this new requirement. Many councils are hiring external consultants to support the roll-out of the new licensing scheme. The cost of this falls firmly at the feet of the landlord through the licensing fee that is now payable.

The argument in favour of licensing is that it creates a more risk-free environment for tenants who share. The arguments against licensing are the costs that are incurred and the time they take to manage. We develop all our HMOs to licensable standards, meaning that there are no surprises later on when the local authority inspect the property: again the detail of this is covered in 'Finish It'. Once the property is completed, the management can be onerous unless you have good systems (covered in 'Future-Proof It').

Licensing involves adherence to local authority guidelines and, since 2018, also imposes minimum room sizes. Only national legislation gives the fundamental rules, and local authorities have interpreted these differently. Some local authorities are more flexible than others in their interpretation of national legislation and combine their licensing policy with housing standards. Fire safety, room sizes and amenities all have to meet minimum standards for any HMO over five rooms. Investigate your local authority rules to ensure yours meets the standards and devise a plan to address these areas if the property doesn't currently meet them. These details should also be addressed in your buildings specification (covered more in 'Finish It').

ARTICLE 4

Article 4 is a restriction to planning permission that was established after a group of residents opposed to the development of HMOs in their area campaigned vigorously to have them disallowed though planning. Current planning regulations state that any building of seven bedrooms or more in size is subject to sui generis planning permission. Under that size, HMOs fall into the C4 (large HMO) use class. Generally, unless article 4 is in place in your local area, you are allowed to take an ordinary property and turn it into an HMO with six rooms or fewer. This is due to permitted development rules that allow certain types of buildings to be developed into other use classes without full planning permission and by a course of action known as prior approval. Article 4 is becoming more prevalent across cities and large conurbations in the UK as HMOs ghettos have exponentially expanded in certain areas (especially student and housing support HMOs).

Before you decide which area to invest in, research your local planning rules and ensure that if you are investing in an article 4 area you will be able to get full planning permission. In addition to article 4, some areas have other planning restrictions that you should investigate as part of your due diligence process. If you do need to apply for full planning permission, a very helpful guide can be found on www.planningportal.co.uk. It is quite possible to apply yourself using the online questionnaire. You will need to include a site plan and a location plan, which you can download from www.siteplan.co.uk or www.buyaplan.co.uk. You will also need scale drawings of the property as it is currently, and in the form in which it is proposed. Using the service of an architect or planning consultant can add value to your application and they will also be able to advise you on the likelihood of your application being passed.

BUILDING REGULATIONS

Building regulations were first introduced into housing design after the great fire of London in 1666, when a rather over-cooked dessert (well it started in Pudding Lane)led to one of the greatest fires to take hold in our capital city. Since then, building regulations have dominated construction design rules for developments and new builds. There are a number of areas of building regulations that affect HMOs, including fire protection, acoustics, water, sewerage and electrical safety.

Your HMO will usually need to conform to building regulations and get a completion certificate for refinancing and for the purposes of the licence, so it's worth understanding exactly what aspects will need to be included in your building specification (covered in more detail in the 'Finish It' chapter). Ensure that your builder has responsibility in the build process for liaison with building control. Most local councils have a building control department but you can also use an independent building control contractor. The normal system for inspections is one at the start of the project to confirm the correct specification and areas of control; an interim inspection to check that work is going to plan and is at the standard required; and a final sign-off meeting to confirm that work has been completed to correct legal standards. Once that has happened, you will receive a building completion certificate in the post. You may find that with certain pieces of work, such as electrical safety, that there are other certificates that your electrician and other trades may issue. The building control officer may wish to see these too to sign off the 'umbrella' building control completion certificate.

HOUSING HEALTH AND SAFETY RATING SYSTEM

The HHSRS is a risk-based assessment tool that is used by environmental health officers to assess the risk (the likelihood and severity) of a hazard in residential housing to the health and safety of occupants or visitors.[6] It is part of overall housing standards and gives local councils clear guidance on what is and what is not acceptable in terms of maintenance and health

6 https://researchbriefings.parliament.uk/ResearchBriefing/Summary/SN01917.

standards in rental property, using a risk-based approach. There is currently a review of the HHSRS being undertaken and this will inform a new set of standard guidelines for landlords.

WIDER SOCIAL AND POLITICAL FACTORS

IMMIGRATION

Since 2004 the UK has had a huge growth in immigration, particularly from the EU. According to the Office for National Statistics, net migration was at a relatively low level during the 1980s and early 1990s. Since 1994, it has been positive every year and rose sharply after 1997. Throughout the 2000s, net migration increased further, partly as a result of immigration of citizens from the countries that joined the EU since 2004 – although after the economic crisis of 2007 this declined. The most commonly stated reason for immigration to the UK is work, with the exception of 2009 to 2012 when formal study was the most common reason. The widening of the European Union to include countries such as Romania and Bulgaria has led to many coming to the UK in the hopes of a better life. Despite the UK's intended exit from the EU, voted for by the British people in 2016, immigration levels continue to remain at a record high. In 2018, net migration stood at 273,000 people. The difference now compared to a decade ago is that we are seeing immigrants from non-EU countries enter the UK on visas and shorter-term working permits. Economic instability, war, unrest and uncertainty, have brought people to the UK where steady and more predictable living standards, coupled with peace and the opportunity of employment, are a strong magnet for migration here. In our HMOs we have had many tenants who are highly qualified GPs, consultants or engineers, but have sacrificed family life back in their own country to search for a steadier and more secure paycheck – much of which is often sent home to support their loved ones.

Patterns of immigration into the UK are fascinating and surprising. It's no surprise that according to Migration Observatory (2019)[7] 'London has the largest number of migrants among all regions of the UK'. However, did you know that (excluding metropolitan counties) the region that has had the biggest growth of immigration over the last decade is Yorkshire and Humber, which has experienced growth of 142%. Scotland is next in line at 135% and coming in third is the East Midlands at 125%. Poland, India and Pakistan are the top three countries of birth for the foreign-born, accounting respectively for 10%, 9% and 6% of the total.

These patterns of movement across the EU and the world have undoubtedly affected the HMO market. Tenants who speak little English, and have no fixed abode, have little option but to find simple, cheap accommodation that is relatively straightforward to rent. With some basic ID and evidence of regular employment, many migrants can only live in HMOs. As the HMO market changes, will we see more services provided for such people? Translation tools, welcome packs, information and advice services – these now need to be at the fingertips of any landlord or agent who is renting to migrants.

7 https://migrationobservatory.ox.ac.uk/resources/briefings/migrants-in-the-uk-an-overview.

EMPLOYMENT LEVELS

You may find it comforting to know that unemployment in the UK currently stands at just 4.4%, which is an incredibly steady backdrop for running HMOs aimed at the working population. Throughout the 18-year period to 2018, unemployment peaked at 8.1% in 2011 and has reduced steadily since then. Despite the turmoil of 2007–8 in the financial markets, the UK regained some level of economic stability over the following decade, which led to sustained high employment. Aside from continuing to be a magnet for immigrants to the UK, this feeds the need for quality accommodation for working people and HMOs provide ideal accommodation for working people who have no dependents. Juggling more than one part-time job has become the norm for many people. So low-cost all-in-one accommodation often provides a win-win for them and their landlord.

MINIMUM WAGE

Evidence seems to suggest that the minimum wage has had a flat-lining effect on the growth of our economy and on the pace of social mobility. Against the rising costs of goods and the underlying rate of inflation (which, although low, has a compound effect like any interest rate application), the minimum wage subtly impacts the economy.

It can mean less opportunity for promotion or increases in salary as employers' wage bills rise each year. One of the problems with static income levels is the reduction in social mobility that this produces. As most economists would concur, a reduction in social mobility leads to diminishing growth across economies.

The likely impacts long term will be overall lower standards of living, which will become the norm and will reduce opportunities. Against the backdrop of a minimum wage, employers are less likely to promote individuals to better paid jobs, and unskilled young people are often overlooked for employment due to the costs of training and upskilling.

In the context of HMOs this could result in the need for more affordable and all-inclusive housing, which is what HMOs offer. It's unlikely that the minimum wage will be abolished any time soon. So, in the meantime, those who live at this income need safe, affordable, clean and comfortable places to live. HMOs are the ideal solution. They may even provide a good incentive to get a pay rise and get out.

TAX CHANGES

Despite proffering no prior warning of this in their manifesto, George Osborne, the then Conservative Chancellor of the Exchequer, decided in 2016 to introduce a brand-new tax regime to the buy-to-let sector. Introduced as a phased approach, landlords who had previously been able to claim all their finance interest costs and other costs (such as insurance, maintenance and repairs, agency fees, etc.) from the income they received from rent were now going to be taxed, such that only 20% would be allowable against income (if they were a higher rate taxpayer). Lower rate taxpayers would not be affected and would still be able to claim 100% of interest relief. However, an additional change would also alter the way that income was calculated, meaning that many more landlords would be pushed into the higher rate band, almost accidentally.

Prior to 2016 changes

Income: £500 per month = £6,000 annual income from property
Outgoings:
£200 mortgage interest
£20 insurance
£50 agency fees
£30 maintenance costs

Profit upon which tax is calculated= £200 pcm

This was the figure that was used to calculate tax. It was a tax on profit, which is the standard way that businesses calculate their taxable income.

Post 2020 changes

After 2020 to calculate taxable profit the mortgage interest must be ignored.

The mortgage interest relief is now replaced by another relief called the "Basic Rate Tax Deduction" which is restricted to 20%. This is applied to the mortgage interest rate cost.

The example to the right highlights that if you are a basic rate tax payer the effect will be the same. You will still pay £60 in tax. However a higher rate tax payer will pay £20 more in tax per month.

(This example assumes the basic rate allowance of £12,500 is already used).

Basic rate tax payers also need to make sure they are not "pushed up" into the higher rate bracket by other income.

	Basic Rate		Higher Rate	
	Pre 2017	Post 2020	Pre 2017	Post 2020
Per Month:	£	£	£	£
Income	500	500	500	500
Outgoings:				
Mortgage Interest:	100	100	100	100
Insurance	20	20	20	20
Agency Fee	50	50	50	50
Maintenance Costs	30	30	30	30
Total Costs	200	200	200	200
Add back non deductible Mortgage interest		100		100
Taxable Profits	**300**	**400**	**300**	**400**
Tax:	**60**	**80**	**120**	**160**
Less Basic Rate Tax Reduction Relief		20		20
Tax Payable:	**60**	**60**	**120**	**140**

In order to prevent yourself from paying too much tax, and to learn what is legally correct tax treatment, you will need to further educate yourself and get professional advice. The important thing to note is that if you are prepared and understand these tax changes, there are ways you can mitigate the impact – and indeed I would recommend you do. Find a qualified and experienced tax accountant to advise you so that you can ensure you are making the most of all the allowances and tax breaks legally afforded you.

Do these changes mean it's no longer worthwhile investing in property? Absolutely not! However, this is why I recommend having a strategy that allows you to move swiftly and deftly – to recognise the need for a sound structure in which to invest and to focus your efforts on the initial goal of creating financial freedom: all of which become possible with a handful of HMOs.

TESTIMONIAL

'When we met Wendy, we already had a couple of HMOs, and a portfolio of single-let properties. We had had some education and been part of a mastermind group, so we felt that we knew what we were doing. Our knowledge about property was sound and we understood building control, licensing rules and housing standards. What we needed was help to leverage our time and implement systems. Within just a few weeks we had already gained more focus and clarity about what we needed to do and we realised how brilliant her mastermind group was compared to others we had been in before. Wendy taught us about systems, processes and tools and, pretty quickly, I (Dave) found that my time working in the business was now time spent *on* the business. This allowed us to do more viewings and find our next HMO.

This next HMO property was one that Wendy came to view with us, and she immediately saw the potential for creating a loft room. After lots of discussion and analysis, we also agreed that going into the loft had definite headroom. We drew up plans and began to convert it. Suddenly our project was getting to a whole new level. After a few weeks of deliberation and planning, we saw the light (literally, as we removed the upper floor of the property to undertake the loft conversion).It was a rather scary time. We weren't sure whether it was Wendy or ourselves who were the most crazy! But we got through it, relatively unscathed, and we now have the most beautiful and amazing six-bed HMO.

It's true we did have quite a lot of knowledge, and I (Dave) had some time to manage the project. But the big-thinking part came from Wendy. Without her, there's no way would have made this amazing project what it is.

Figures:
Purchase price £81,000
Legals and fees £2,000
Stamp duty £2,430
Refurb £50,000
Refinance cost £2,000
Cost of finance £6,500
Estimated revaluation £150,000
Cash left in £23,838
Cashflow £28,080

Yearly net profit £10,500
Yield 19%
ROI 44% (based on PP)'
Sue Ayton and Dave Oldroyd
http://www.qualityyorkshirehomes.co.uk/

THE FIVE-STEP SYSTEM

CHAPTER 5

THE SYSTEM

'You never change things by fighting the existing reality. To change something, build a new model that makes the existing model obsolete.'
—R. Buckminster Fuller

I've always found a complicated dish easier to make if I have a recipe and taking an ordinary property to turn into an HMO can often feel like you're making a gastronomic feast. It was a few years ago that I decided to simplify this process. It meant I could categorise all our systems easily and quickly and, in turn, scale up our business more efficiently. I realised that having a recipe would help other people to follow too. So, this Five-Step System is what we use, and what I now teach others to use.

If you are aiming to get five HMOs to reach your goal of financial freedom, then using a system will be key to the pace at which you can implement and scale up. Whether you are a novice investor or have already got some experience, if you follow the system you can make £1,000 profit per property per month. This is five times the usual profit on a single buy-to-let property. Not only is the income far greater, but the risk of voids is far lower, as you will usually have at least some of the rooms rented out, if not all. There are considerations for you as you enter this market: whether or not you rent fully-inclusive of bills; whether you invest in licensed or unlicensed HMOs; and which section of the market you intend to address. This section will help you think through all these decisions so that you are educated and informed about this lucrative investment opportunity.

THE FIVE-STEP SYSTEM

1. Find It
2. Fund It
3. Finish It
4. Fill It
5. Future-Proof It

In my previous book, I outlined the system and gave tips for each one, but I was bombarded with requests to go into more detail. One lady very kindly gave me this feedback: 'Wendy, your book is outstanding – so easy to read, full of useful tips and practical to implement. The problems is, there's not enough of it. I would love to read more from your experience, your examples and stories and your knowledge. When is the next book coming out?'

This section describes in much greater detail the Five-Step System and will give you a firm foundation for your own HMO business. Each step is broken down piece by piece so that you can easily and quickly understand what is needed for each step to be thorough and complete. It also means you can manage a refurbishment project alongside finding your next property.

Throughout the section I will mention some of the online tools we use to enable us to manage these steps. But tools are changing all the time. You may find there are ones you are more naturally drawn to than others and there are many that will do the job really well. Find the tools that help you execute the steps and stick to them. Using these five steps will help you quickly and easily know what you need to do and in what order. It won't be long before you're giving in your notice and travelling the world!

RESTARTING THE HMO ENGINE

Earlier, I told you about my initial HMO – the very first property I bought way back in 1996. That was the student multilet that ended up becoming a family rental. Time passed and I had invested in a number of single buy-to-lets since that stuttering start. I was convinced that I didn't have what it took to do HMOs, so I steered away from them. The Spring of 2012 saw all that change. The combination of yearning for something more with the pain of not yet having it ate away at me. I had read Robert Kiyosaki's book and had renewed energy and vision. I had by that time made the decision that I had to re-enter the HMO market and so, tentatively, I booked a viewing on a property that could be a perfect small (mini) HMO. It was July 2012. And it was a perfect day to attempt something new. The sun was shining and all was good with the world. I woke up feeling nervous yet excited. I knew what lay ahead of me that day could be the start of something big – something I had hoped for – yet had never materialised. My whole life I had been trying to make things work by combining my passion for doing something deeply worthwhile and fulfilling with the ability to make serious income. After years of wrestling with these two values – money and mission – I had come to the realisation that I could achieve both. I just needed to choose the right domain. Although I had been investing small-time in property, I hadn't focused my efforts. I had been running my handful of single buy-to-lets alone and managing pretty well. But I was ready to grow. I felt it deep within my soul.

The nation was recovering from one of the worst financial shocks of all time (the crash of 2008) and lenders were becoming slightly less cautious about buy-to-let again. Finance was available and my handful of single buy-to-lets meant that I was eligible for mortgages for an HMO.

On this particular summer's day, I took my youngest son into nursery and dropped the other boys off at school. I drove a few miles west to Crewe. This was my investing area where there was a steady demand from tenants for family homes. My portfolio was plodding along and the repayment mortgages were all being paid down. It was tortoise-like. Slow and steady. I pulled up outside a two-bedroom terraced house. I could see the estate agent's car parked slightly further down the road, so I knew I was in the right place. There was no for sale sign up outside the house, just a neat hedge and a welcoming clean and white front door. I rang the bell and the door opened.

My jaw dropped. The lady standing on the threshold was none other than the financial accountant with whom I had worked at the council a few years before. We had sat literally opposite each other at work and knew each other pretty well. She had recently met the man of her dreams and was getting married, so no longer needed her property. They were buying somewhere together so her terraced house was surplus to requirements. As I looked around the house, it was a fairly standard two-bed terrace house. Two reception rooms downstairs, two bedrooms, a kitchen and a bathroom. It was in reasonably good condition and on the market for £79,000. The boiler seemed in good order, and all the windows were double-glazed. All the expensive, invisible jobs that cost money but don't add any obvious lettable value to the property were done. The interior of the house was a bit tired, but nothing that a lick of paint couldn't rectify, and the bathroom was a good size. I was hooked. I thanked her for her time and asked what had happened to the estate agent. 'I don't know' she said. 'Maybe she was doing a viewing at another property locally'? It had been useful to have Pauline show me around. I could ask her more about the costs of running the property, such as the council tax band and a rough estimate of water costs and utilities. I knew that the utility costs would change if I turned it into an HMO, but I was trying to build rapport to assess how much I could offer on the deal. I had heard of people buying properties below market value and thought that if I could try some persuasion tactics I might be able to get this property BMV. It was also useful to get the insider knowledge direct from the vendor as estate agents often don't know the story or facts that prove invaluable when you start to negotiate. The problem was that Pauline already knew me, so she could see when I was getting into 'price and bottom line' suggestion-mode. We finished the viewing, I thanked her and said goodbye and all the best for her upcoming wedding.

As I drove home, I pondered the viewing. The house seemed ideal. It was in a great area – close to Crewe's mainline railway station and the town centre. All the rooms were a good size. The refurbishment wouldn't cost too much as I didn't need to put in a new kitchen or bathroom. It was minor redecoration and some small reconfigurations that were needed. I decided to put in an offer. At that point my plan for financing the deal was to cash in an old endowment policy that we were paying for each month, yet was due to return about 3% on top of the capital we had invested. Overall the return was lamentable. If I made 10% return on this HMO, it was triple what this endowment policy was making me. So I called the estate agent and put in a really cheeky offer: £76,000. That to me at that time was a cheeky offer. Since then I'm glad to say I have learned a lot more about buying properties BMV. I was shocked when I got a call half an hour later to say the vendor had rejected my offer. Perhaps knowing the vendor had not been to my benefit after all. I wondered what Pauline must be thinking now. That her old boss was being cheeky? Well, why change the habit of a lifetime? In reality, this was still a reasonable offer but she had her bottom line. She couldn't accept any less than £78,000.

If I had known then what I know now, I would have suggested a number of other options that she may have taken up – such as a lease option, delayed completion or vendor finance. All strategies that are legal yet creative and allow you to secure properties without having a mortgage or having a lengthy transaction process. At the time I was almost totally uneducated in property despite already having some houses in my portfolio. And clearly my ninja persuasion techniques had fallen on deaf ears. The house was ideal for what I wanted to do, and there were very few others available. The stock of properties for sale had diminished since the crash, and sellers were very protective about values and the price they would accept. I was confident that even though £78,000 was in no way a 'deal' it was still a chance for me to get started on my next step – creating a portfolio of cashflowing HMOs. So, I phoned back the estate agent and offered her acceptable price of £78,000. Strangely enough, it was accepted.

Four weeks later, I was the proud owner of a two-up two-down, ready for alteration and adaptation into a fantastic HMO. I found a good local builder (who was the husband of a good friend of mine) and was also a master joiner with all the trades at his disposal. With a comprehensive plan written on half a piece of A4 paper, he set about creating my HMO. I was heavily involved with the refurb – visiting the project almost every day in the beginning, and sourcing many of the items needed. The house benefitted from space either side of the chimney breasts was large enough to build-in a wardrobe with storage above. This made great use of the space and reduced the length of my furniture shopping list. After about four weeks of refurbishment the house was ready for furnishing, and I was flushed with the result.

After what felt like days of shopping and deliveries, I spent a whole weekend putting together flat-pack furniture. The problem was after the first couple of hours I was exhausted. So that evening I bribed my eldest boys to give up the rest of their weekend to come and help me. They agreed. So, with electric screwdrivers at the ready, and Radio 1 blaring through the iPod speakers, the family gathered round me to finish our very first HMO. The boys were brilliant – they painted and decorated, constructed endless flat-packs, and unpacked and arranged all the cutlery, crockery and cuisinery! On the Sunday night we downed tools and stood back to look around the house. Once the plastic wrapping was taken away and the mattresses were on the beds, with just another half hour's effort the rooms were dressed and ready. We were very tired, but satisfied. As I walked round the house I had a good feeling. It was a home. It was bijou but beautiful. The furniture was good quality, the built-in wardrobes gave excellent storage, and the carpets and curtains matched. I even had colour-coordinated cushions on the beds. I was happy and I thanked the boys in a way that most teenagers understand best – cash in hand. They were now very happy too. I was on the verge of the unknown. What was needed now was to take photos and start advertising the rooms. Within a fortnight the rooms were let. I calculated my cashflow on this little, mediocre and insignificant property.

Monthly Figures

Rental income = £1,340
Outgoings –
Mortgage = £240
Utilities = £150
Insurance = £30
Cleaner = £40 (twice monthly)
Broadband = £35
Council tax = £90
Total outgoings = £585
Profit =£755

I couldn't believe it. From a simple house that would have been a single buy-to-let, I'd done it. I'd created this HMO from scratch and now there was no looking back. With nearly £760 profit per month, I was convinced that I could make this work. My dream of financial freedom, where I had the choice to leave my job if I wanted to, was becoming real. Previous to this, I had been wary about believing the promises of others who touted claims from following this or that strategy. I questioned in my mind whether they had the constraints that I did – children, caring responsibilities, a partner working away from home all week, no money to invest with? I read voraciously and attended lots of webinars. It began to dawn on me that these speakers were no different from me, yet they had taken different action. They had taken calculated and educated risks. They had gone further and deeper, and thus had accelerated their journey. This was what I wanted too. At the age of 43, I was no spring chicken and I was conscious that time was running out. I wanted to know more and grow more. And the time was *now*.

If you're wondering how you can start, this might just be the kind of HMO you can start with. A 'beta' project as my husband neatly termed it – one on which you cut your teeth and learn the ropes. If you make this kind of profit too, you'll find the bug will bite. If you are starting out with a small pot of money and want to learn the process of refurbishment, tenanting and running an HMO, a four-bed project could be ideal. (Check your local authority planning rules. If you are investing in an article 4 area you will still need planning permission for any size of HMO.) At the present time, it will not require a licence, although I would suggest you still invest in fire-proofing the house for safety. It's a great mini-mo project in which you can hone your skills and de-risk your investment.

After developing this simple four-bed HMO I was impatient for more. I found a large three-bed terraced house which I turned into a seven-bed HMO (more of that project later). What I learned was that waiting for everything to be right in my life before I took action was never going to happen. There is never an ideal time to get started – *never*. Waiting for the right time will put you where I was in my wilderness years – wandering in the desert and wondering how you got there. You have to make the decision, commit to taking action and *go for it*.

Over the next few projects I learned the details about investing in HMOs. From legislation to licensing, from ASTs to acoustics, and from refurbs to rentals. No stone was left unturned! By learning each detail of starting, scaling and systemising the business, I realised how much I had learned in a very short time, and how much this could help other people.

Creating a Five-Step System helped me to simplify the process and enabled me to scale the business much faster. I realised how much easier it was once I had a clear process to follow. So, here for you is my simple Five-Step System. Broken down in the following chapters, you will learn everything you need to know to create extraordinary profits from ordinary properties.

If you've made the decision to say yes – then here's the detail to make it happen.

TESTIMONIAL

'When I started to work with Wendy, I had already had a handful of buy-to-let properties. This small portfolio was performing adequately but not really creating exciting income for me. As you can probably tell from my photo, I am not from the UK. In fact, I am from Japan and my family still lives there. I wanted to help my family back home by making money from property investing, but it wasn't happening fast enough. The other problem I had was that I had very little money left to invest with. So,

I was a bit slow and I was really stuck. I joined Wendy's mentoring programme and it really helped me grow. I found a business partner who also pushed me way out of my comfort zone and we set up a company to invest in HMOs. Using what I learnt from Wendy, I started to use other people's money straight away and bought my very first HMO. I copied her system and learned how to refurbish and 'stage' my property (which I really have to thank my wife, Linda, for). Now I have a number of HMOs all cashflowing and making me great money every month. The best thing is that this has led to so many other opportunities and helped me to even bigger projects. I really can say that meeting Wendy at the time I did was life-changing and I will forever be grateful to her.'

Taro Nabetani

CHAPTER 6

FIND IT

'Success is where preparation and opportunity meet'
—Bobby Unser. American car racing expert

One of the most common questions I get asked by people looking to invest in HMOs is 'Where should I invest?' This is an important question to answer as ideally, you want to choose an area that gives you the opportunity to develop a portfolio of HMOs. Being able to leverage your knowledge, contacts, time and money creates compound growth for the future, and wealth building through assets such as HMOs works better when you are committed to growing your portfolio over time. You will be able to achieve fast cashflow with HMOs but, if you also want to create wealth that outlasts your life, then assets need to be bought and held. Finding the right place to invest in HMOs is therefore a pretty crucial question to be addressed, for only then can you leverage the contacts, trades and market knowledge you have gleaned.

Many investors are attracted to the idea of long-term passive income through bricks and mortar, without realising that market forces are as important as the product, which in this case is a room in a shared house. The context in which we invest today was covered in more depth in section 1, so I will not repeat myself here, except to add that continual learning of the systems that impact you as an investor will help you hugely to navigate the HMO waters we are all sailing, and which can often be more than a little choppy.

This moment in the property investing cycle offers fantastic opportunities if you know what you're doing; if you're prepared to adopt advanced tools to save time and money; and if you understand the market. There really is no time to lose and no time like the present.

FINDING THE RIGHT AREA

As is true with many other areas of our lives where we seek further clarity, the answer can be discovered by further, better questions. You may for example ask yourself:

- What is my overall goal?
- Where do I want to be in three years' time?
- Who do I need to help me?
- What kind of returns am I looking for?
- Are my expectations realistic?
- Will I use my own capital (cash) to invest or will I use other people's money?
- Am I going to manage the property myself?
- Do I have other experience I can utilise to grow this business?
- What are the skills I bring to this business?
- What are my initial goals in terms of income (profit) and how much time will I be able to give to developing

my HMOs?
- Am I looking for capital growth and/or cashflow?
- Do I fully understand the Five-Step Process to take an ordinary house and turn it into an HMO?
- Who do I know and who else do I need?
- Whose advice might I need along the way?

Once you are clearer about your goals and expectations you will start to clarify whether your HMOs need to be in the north or south of the country, whether you are aiming at students, professionals or LHA (housing benefit), and what kind of property will suit your chosen HMO strategy. Research that I carried out for my previous book, and that I repeat here to emphasise the point, is that HMOs will work in most areas of the UK. Knowing your local area is crucial to understanding the wider market and gives you confidence when changes are afoot in the broader economy. Investing in property is usually a long-term activity and therefore being relatively certain of a market for the next five years will give you a level of certainty. Nothing is predictable though, especially when it's about the future so this list is here to help you just to minimise risk. You can never eliminate it entirely.

- What are the local transport links like in the area?
- Local plan – what are the proposed developments and regeneration plans if any?
- What kinds of employment are available locally? Where are the big employers located?
- Where are the local amenities?
- Can you buy a pint of milk within a five-minute walk (the 'pint of milk rule')?
- What is the local social classification and demography?
- Are the houses nearby owner-occupied or rented? What

is the proportion of each?
- How much housing stock is there within a half-mile radius? How many are currently on the market?
- What do three local estate agents say about the market locally? Buoyant, flat, in decline?
- Is this an article 4 area? Are there any restrictive licensing rules?
- What are the average rental levels?
- What are the average room rental amounts?
- Get three comparables from the local area of sold prices.
- What is the target market? Can I evidence demand?

There are definitely some core indicators that make certain areas preferential for getting good all-round returns. After further research and discussion with HMO investors across the UK, I have slightly refined these indicators.

My refined indicators are:
- A population of *no less* than 80,000 people – otherwise you are unlikely to have the right number and supply of houses.
- Robust and various transport links to the wider region (train, coach, bus, motorway, tram etc.).
- Within 15 miles of another equally large conurbation.
- At least 10 medium to large employers (3,000 people plus) who have a significant need for skilled or semi-skilled labour.
- Local plans for growth, regeneration and investment (this is not always easy to uncover but looking at the local plan will ascertain local trends for housing and employment. Knowing the priorities of your local council

for development over the next five years is a core part of understanding the viability of a potential HMO.)

- Retail and shopping facilities that cater for all segments of the population.
- At least 10–15% of property in the rental market (i.e. predictable and steady rental market). This is true in most areas of the UK at present. This factor is important as it influences your tenants' ability to move up and out of your HMO eventually. Some may leave due to job changes; others will purchase their own property and many will move into a single-let property. If there is limited opportunity to move up the rental ladder this will affect the popularity of the area with regard to HMO room lets. Also having a strong local rental demand will ensure there are plenty of lettings agents locally who you can work with to let out rooms.
- Supply and demand of tenants.

HMOs are more time-consuming and more labour-intensive in the first few months than single buy-to-lets. The refurbishment often takes longer and the complications can be more exacting. There are additional levels of housing regulations to be conformed to and there are more detailed questions about the safety arrangements and licensing certification that you'll be asked to answer. Does this mean that HMOs are impossible unless you live within five miles of them? Not at all. You just have to be more organised than if you did live close-by. I advise all investors to have a great dream team (or power team) – this includes a reliable builder, project manager and, of course, managing agent. Although the practical issues often take a back seat when deciding your ideal investment area, and the numbers seem to be the only features doing the talking, it's highly valuable to consider the practical access to your chosen location early on.

I believe you will maximise your chances of success if you create a portfolio of five or more HMOs in an area no wider than 20 square miles. An appropriate way to start is to find a location within an hour from where you live. I was lucky that I lived close to two areas that proved to be ripe for investing in high-end HMOs. As I was a busy mum with four boys to look after, I had no choice but to invest somewhere local to where I lived, saving myself time and travel. I have worked with investors who have stressful and demanding full-time jobs and invest over 200 miles from where they live. They couldn't do this without support and a good team though. It certainly is possible to invest further afield but your priorities will be to find a great team, and to concentrate your efforts on one area. Get five properties up and running first before you expand into other areas or apply other strategies.

The task of choosing *where* to invest depends on a number of factors. Doing your due diligence now and tracking your research will help you later when you come to raising finance. Piece together your research and make an educated decision. Too many investors miss out this vital piece of work and then find later that they can't rent their rooms or they have spent far too much on the refurbishment. I'd suggest that you create a spreadsheet to track and gather your data from this exercise (you can get a downloadable copy of this from www.centreround.co.uk).

1. Create a number of columns entitled Postcode Area, Average House Price, Median Property Type, Average Sale Price, Average Length of Time to Sell. You can get

all this information from www.home.co.uk. You also want a column on Notes on Locality and Type of Tenant.

2. Identify two or three potential areas within an hour or maximum of hour and a half from where you live. Clarify the postcode areas that you will be focusing on. Be as specific as you can.
    - Identify the *macro* forces in the local housing stock, namely average house price sale over the last 12 months
    - Median *type* of property (three-bed semi, two-bed terrace etc.)
    - Average sale price for three-bed terrace or semi
    - Average length of time to sell
    - A couple of useful websites for this exercise are www.home.co.uk and www.mouseprice.co.uk. Put your results into your spreadsheet.
3. Visit the local council's website and download the local plan. Make a coffee, sit down at your PC and determine to take the time to understand the potential developments, sites, new conurbations, housing estates, infrastructure projects and housing policy that the local council will be implementing over the next few years. This will be invaluable advice as you 'future-proof' your investment. It will allow you to see where growth is likely to occur and where new employers may spring up.
4. Drill down into your chosen postcode areas with www.streetchecker.com to assess the types of tenants who currently reside there. This tool will also give an overview of crime stats and demographic groups. Your tenants are likely to be blue-collar workers who are in demographic group C–D who are aged between 21 and 55. Look for evidence that your areas have a solid

attraction for this type of person.

5. Buy a large Ordnance Survey Explorer map that you can open up and spread out on your floor or kitchen table. It needs to be a map that covers at least 20 miles squared as this will provide sufficient detail to answer more of the questions you want to answer. Online maps are fine, but nothing beats a physical map upon which you can circle potential areas and highlight these significant features of your chosen investing area. Use a Google search to identify large local employers, city and town maps and transport routes, access into and out of the central area, hospitals, shopping centres and so on. (You could notate your findings on your spreadsheet.)
6. What is the population growth for this location? (You can get this information from your local council or the Office for National Statistics – www.ons.gov.uk). What is the likelihood of further growth in the area? Combined with the evidence from the local plan which will tell you where larger developments and investments will be taking place, you can predict with some accuracy what the shape of the population will look like in 3–5 years' time.
7. Next, you need to look at demand and supply for rooms. This is much harder to be accurate as it depends on information that is unverifiable. Spareroom.co.uk is a valuable tool but won't give you a full picture as many adverts and tenant profiles are out-of-date. However, this is the best place to start to get an idea of demand and supply.

SUPPLY AND DEMAND

Here is a miniguide to gathering core data about supply and demand (more detail on this can be found on my YouTube channel: https://www.youtube.com/user/wendywl).

1. Log into Spareroom and search on 'Rooms Available' in your chosen location.
2. Drill down into 'map' view to ascertain exactly where they are (postcodes often cover wide search areas).
3. Sort the types of rooms using the search buttons on the left (e.g. how many en-suite rooms for professionals are available? You might find there is a sparsity of competition for higher level rooms).
4. Now, search on 'Flatmates' for potential tenants. Identify the maximum rents being budgeted by your potential tenants. Ask yourself the following questions about what you see:
    - What amenities are being asked for by tenants but not being provided by the current rooms available?
    - How many people are looking compared to the number of applicable rooms available? I work on a 3:2 ratio of tenants to rooms.
5. Is there a higher ratio of those looking than rooms that are available? (Bear in mind that many house adverts have expired and are languishing in an effort to create a steady stream of interested tenants – even though the house may be currently full).

The answer to these questions will give you a good insight into local supply and demand. Next, I'd suggest looking on Rightmove for property that is available at the average room rent being offered by the rooms on Spareroom. How many adverts are there and what are the rents? What is the quality of the rooms on offer? Could you produce higher quality rooms and service than you see?

DATA ANALYSIS

Having gathered your data, the question you need to ask is 'what does it tell me?' Is there a sizeable working population of the right demographic? Is there local growth? Is transport provision sufficient? Are house prices relative to rents going to produce a good yield? Is there sufficient spread between lower and higher value properties such that I can add enough value?

As someone who rather enjoys finding out information, I find the process of research to be fun and motivating. Gathering data like this can cause unintended consequences though. Have you ever heard the phrase 'analysis paralysis'? If so, you'll understand that depending on your personal reaction to data and facts, too much data gathering will not inspire you to take action. It will have the opposite effect of paralysing you with indecision.

The second unintended consequence is that you will be overwhelmed with choice, as you recognise that *all* the places on your shortlist suddenly could become HMO hotspots. You suddenly find yourself tuning into the news when the presenter announces that a piece about Ipswich town centre's redevelopment is about to be aired. Or a visit to your second cousin who you've not seen for six years suddenly becomes terribly attractive now that you remember she lives in Hull. Your eldest son who's about to make his university choices is persuaded by you to visit Preston as you've heard they have a renowned course in your son's chosen subject. His suspicions about your motivation are confirmed when you reassure him that he has plenty of time to explore the university at his own pace (while you sneak off to do some local property viewings).

To overcome indecision, procrastination and being overwhelmed, I would recommend that you set yourself a window in which to determine where your specific HMO investment area will be. Study the data, decide on an area and start booking some viewings.

Until you make the decision to say yes, you'll stay in no-man's-HMO-land forever. I am not trying to be flippant, but you will not find a perfect HMO hotspot. All of those have already been taken. What you might find though is an area ripe for future development, where growth is occurring and there is a definite need for higher quality housing. My approach has always been to buck the trend and create a product (a room) that is delicious to the eye and to the senses. This creates interest and desire from your customer.

FINDING THE RIGHT PROPERTY

The best properties to convert into HMOs are those with regular and larger rooms (ensuring they meet legal minimum room sizes), houses that may already need some work to bring them to modern standards; and houses you can add value to by converting them. Commercial properties can be converted into HMOs, including offices and shops too. It is possible to buy a standard family property in a relatively good condition and turn it into an HMO quickly and cheaply. However, you might find you face some drawbacks to this approach:

- Refinancing might be challenging as there is not enough that you have changed to add value and therefore get money out of the property.
- Fit-for-purpose. If the refurb is not substantial enough to meet the needs of your tenant market, you will not be able to maintain standards and rent rooms consistently.
- Purchase price is likely to be higher than with a house that is already in need of some TLC.
- If you do decide to add en-suites, change the kitchen and redecorate, the price of these additions can add up to more than the value of the property once completed.

A good way to start is to look for a house that is large enough to have at least four or five lettable bedrooms (these could include downstairs reception rooms), a decent communal area and kitchen (this could be a kitchen diner) and the ability to support HMO infrastructure – a sound heating system with enough hot water; plentiful electrical sockets and enough amenities to ensure the tenants' comfort. In our area we find that Victorian terraced houses work well, as they have the space and layout that is ideal. I have seen many other types of building work extremely well as HMOs: flats above shops divided into three or more lettable rooms; an old dentist's surgery converted into six spacious rooms with en-suites and two shared kitchens; a new three-storey townhouse; a pub split into two six-bed HMOs. There are any number of possibilities once you understand the parameters.

SOURCING METHODS

There are a number of ways you can find property that will work as an HMO:

1. **Estate agents and lettings agents.** There is a perception that agents don't want to work with investors, but I have found the opposite to be true. By being polite, respectful, returning calls and following up with them, you can create a win-win-win for yourself, the vendor and the agent. I don't agree with those who side-step agents' fees when they are introduced to a vendor by an agent, with whom they then negotiate a creative deal. Make it worth the agent's while and you'll find they will call you first whenever they have a problem property that can't sell at the vendor's asking price. Agents are busy people and would rather work with someone who is a serious buyer, who is professional and respectful and not an egomaniac. Arrive on time for a viewing, be prepared, don't waste the time of the viewing person (who may be on a tight deadline – if necessary, arrange a follow-up viewing), and give feedback when requested. Our motto is 'treat others the way you want to be treated' and, if you adopt that approach, you'll find that you will soon develop a healthy and profitable business partnership.
2. **Your local network.** When you develop a regular presence in your chosen investment area and get known for what you do, you will find people will approach you with property problems, including properties that aren't selling. Many of these 'problems' can be solved with a creative approach such as lease options, delayed completion, vendor finance deals and other creative

solutions, which are beyond the scope of this book. Suffice to say that even if you're looking for a three-bed terrace to turn into your first five-bed HMO, local people are one of the best sources of information and contacts. Take a walk around the neighbourhood, talk to the people in the street, in corner shops and takeaways. If you let them know what you're looking for, and that there is an incentive for them if they lead you to a good deal, you'll find they will perk up and begin to rack their brains for knowledge of any property that might help you. Being seen and known in your area is key to using your network effectively.

3. **Direct-to-vendor advertising.** Using a variety of means such as postcards in local shops and takeaways, leafleting, and advertising in local papers you can get some great leads from people who want to sell their property but for various reasons have chosen not to put them up for sale with an agent. One of the simplest and most automatic methods that takes the least of your time is leafleting. By creating a simple leaflet that you can have delivered regularly, you will soon become known locally for what you do and what you're looking for. There are templates that you can use (see further resources section for more information) to ensure that all your key information is included, and a call to action is added. Ensure you engage with a leaflet delivery company too after you've agreed your delivery area – you don't want to deliver the leaflets yourself!
4. **Council lists**. Your local council is required to keep a list of empty properties. Find the department that manages this and get onto their email marketing list. Another department worth connecting with is the one

that liaises with other local landlords – often this is the private sector housing team. They may have an accreditation scheme and run regular training courses where you can meet local landlords. Many of the landlords at these events have been in the industry a long time and may be looking for help with their portfolio. Make contact with the council and get connected to the people who know others in your area who may be looking for help or the fresh blood of a new investor.

5. **Websites and social media.** In addition to traditional sources of marketing you need to develop your social media presence and your internet presence to tell people what you do and how you can help them. Within our business, we've found that our social media presence has become more powerful in creating leads than traditional media. Having a Facebook profile and an up-to-date website is crucial to engage people with what you do and how you do it. Create a strategy for posting material regularly to let people see that you are activeand also be clear about what you are looking for. Enable people to contact you easily by adding a 'Contact Us' button on your page or website.
6. **Auctions**. There are without doubt many bargains to be had in a property auction, but you need to be careful about doing your due diligence beforehand. You should always download the legal pack from the website and ideally get a solicitor to check over the documentation. You need to ensure you have your finances in order and have completed the auctioneer's information before so that you can bid. The trap that many people fall into is the emotional roller coaster that happens at an auction. It's extremely easy to get carried away once bidding on

your chosen lot begins. Other people start to bid just as the auctioneer raises the emotional temperature by emphasising the speed of the sale. The auctioneer takes further bids to close the lot, and, simultaneously, you're craning your neck to keep up with what is happening in the room. It's very easy to keep adding another £500 or £1,000 to what you had considered your ceiling price to be and find that when the gavel falls, you've sealed the deal *but* you've paid too much for the property. With an auction you are legally bound to complete the sale within a certain time, so being prepared to buy speedily is vital.

My preferred option is to watch the properties that are listed at auction and, if the guide price appears to offer a genuine opportunity (which is often set at 10% of the acceptable reserve price that the property can be sold at), I will make a pre-auction offer. This can buy you more time and allow you to purchase with a mortgage more easily. Another approach is to buy post-auction if the property doesn't sell. Post-auction the vendor may be suitably disappointed that the property didn't sell and is now willing to take a lower offer. One piece of advice I would give is to go and view an auction prior to buying a property through an auction. Once you understand how it works and how it feels you will be far more prepared if you do decide to buy at an auction.

The following questions can help you gather useful information about a property:

- How long has the property been on the market?
- Why does the vendor want to sell?
- Is the vendor motivated to sell quickly or open to a

creative solution?
- History of the house and any surveys completed?
- Have any environmental reports or prior valuations been done?
- Do you have plans and a layout for the property?
- Where is the boundary of the title?
- What is the parking situation like?
- Is the property freehold or leasehold?
- Are there any service charges or ground rents to pay?
- Do you have a complete set of photos?

Over 80% of our deals have been done with estate agents and the majority of people who want to sell their houses will list them with an agent. As you continue educating yourself and learning more about property you will be able to learn about lease options, delayed completion, vendor finance, probate sales and adverse possession.

DUE DILIGENCE

'Learn to use your emotions to think,
not think with your emotions.'
—Robert T. Kiyosaki, *Rich Dad, Poor Dad*

When I was about 14 years old, I was asked out on a first date by a local boy who seemed rather nice. I was flattered by his attentions. He was a couple of years older than me and lived a few streets away. I'd met him at my church's youth club and we liked the same music and had similar interests. He was a few inches taller than me and attractive. All my friends were clearly impressed that I'd been asked out by him, so I saw no reason to turn him down!

When my dad found out, it was a rather different matter though. 'What school does he go to? What do his parents do for a living? Has he had other girlfriends before? Does he ride a motorbike? Does he intend to buy a motorbike?'. As a parent myself now, I can see exactly where my dad was coming from, but at the time I just thought he was *way* over the top. I was only dating this guy, not planning to marry him and settle down with a mortgage and three kids!

What my dad was doing was what many parents of teenagers want to do – due diligence. Finding out what he could before any sign of commitment started to rear its head. Understanding the suitability of the match before it could go any further. As it was, we lasted a few dates until my own internal antenna told me this was never gonna be a long-term relationship. Especially when he told me he supported West Ham …

Your internal antenna is a good predictor of many things, but in all my years of buying property, the one thing it doesn't do too well at is property due diligence. This is because we buy as if we were going to live in the house, as if we were going to enjoy the interiors, as if we were parking our car outside. This is a dangerous approach because your tenants may be very different from you and have a very different lifestyle. Being able to be objective and assess the whole project from a number of standpoints is really important so that you don't launch forth without really understanding the risks. You need to buy with your head not with your heart.

CONDITION OF THE PROPERTY

You will probably undertake a full refurb of the house but it's worth noting that some of the issues picked up by your due diligence will be 'invisible and expensive' and others will be 'visible and add value' corrections. A few useful tools to have with you when conducting viewing are: a damp metre (a cheap handheld tool you can buy on eBay to check damp levels); a spirit level to check evenness of surfaces; a laser measuring device that can calculate floor area as well as measure widths and lengths; and a drone for overhead shots of the property. Take plenty of camera and video footage to record all aspects of the house that you can analyse further later.

Buying a house with invisible corrections means that you won't necessarily see that translate into an uplift in value.

- Structure – does the house feel straight? Are there any signs of previous movement – cracks, flooring that is not horizontal, external signs of misalignment? (I would always advise a survey that will pick this up anyway.)
- External render and brickwork – is it sound and in good condition or will it need replacing or repairing or repointing?
- Roof – does the condition look good? Is it level and are there any tiles missing? Make sure the flashings and the fascias are secure and in good condition. How does the chimney stack look?
- Gutters and drains – are they clear of debris and in good condition? Are they securely attached to the property?
- Walls – are any of the external walls bowed and is the pointing in good condition? What is the condition of the internal walls?

- Ceilings – are there cracks and bows in the ceiling? Do the ceilings have signs of damp or water ingress? This may point to a leak from the roof, bathroom or external gutter.
- Doors – do all doors close properly? If not, it could be a sign of structural movement.
- Cracks – check all rooms and hallways for cracks. If you are able to fit the side of a 10p into the crack, there could by a structural problem that will require further investigation.
- Boiler – is there central heating and does the boiler and all radiators appear to be in good condition? A new heating system will cost around £3k or more depending on the size of the property.
- Electrics – do the sockets and consumer unit look old or do they look modern and in good condition? Will you need to upgrade?
- Windows – is there double glazing? Open and check the windows, as they can also be expensive to replace, and make notes if the property is only part double glazed. What is the condition of the front and back door?
- Flooring – does any part of the floor creek or feel bouncy and are the carpets, tiles, lino in good condition?
- Damp – there are many different types of damp and only a specialist will be able to tell you the cause and cure when you first start out. But it's important to check for any signs of damp. If the property is furnished, it's a good idea to look behind the furniture and make sure you check the ceilings and not just the walls. Damp often gives out a particular smell. Check for patches of mould and condensation.

ASSESS THE DEAL

Crunching the numbers on your HMO before you start is a vital part of the analysis to decide whether this is a worthwhile project to undertake. Careful planning, analysis and execution will mean that you get your figures right and will mean that you have some room for contingencies if and when variances occur. There are five key aspects to financial due diligence:

- Cost of project including refurbishment
- Value of project once complete
- Income
- Expenditure (including mandatory licensing costs)
- Returns

For example:
You find a three-bed property on the market for £140,000. It has two large reception rooms and a dated kitchen. There is a family bathroom upstairs and a downstairs toilet.

Using the floor plans and the information you have gleaned (and with the friendly help of a local builder) you're able to predict that the cost of the refurb will be around £39,000. This will include en-suites in three of the upstairs rooms, a conversion of the downstairs WC into a shower room, a new kitchen and an update to the central heating system, redecoration throughout and furniture and furnishings. Your research tells you that market room rents in your area for a double room are £420 per month and with an en-suite are £450 per month. The project will be delivering five double beds, including three that are en-suites. You'll be buying this with a buy-to-let mortgage and refinancing onto a commercial HMO mortgage afterwards. This already gives you a good idea about the potential income and return you'll get on this project.

When calculating the costs of a project remember to include the financial borrowing cost if you are buying the property with a mortgage. (For a detailed cost and project analysis spreadsheet please go to www.centreround.co.uk.) You can then enter your own figures into this downloadable spreadsheet for a more accurate picture.

(A quick note on stamp duty. Whilst writing this book a new ruling came into place to do with stamp duty. We are awaiting further clarification, but it seems that any property that is uninhabitable on the point of purchase is ineligible for stamp duty. For further clarification on this you should consult your solicitor or accountant.)

Cost of project
Purchase price: £130,000
Made up of
    Deposit: £32,500
    Mortgage: £97,500
Stamp duty: £4,000
Finance costs (over six months @ 4% interest):£1,950
Project costs:
    Refurb cost: £39,000
    Contingency: £4,000
Total cost:
Your input: £81,450
Mortgage: £97,500
Total:£178,950

Broken down into cost per lettable room (a very useful

comparison figure) = total cost of project/ number of rooms = £178,950/five = £35,790

Income
Three rooms @ £450 per month
Two rooms @ £420 per month
Monthly income = £2,190

Expenditure
Mortgage payment:£325 (before refinancing)
Insurance: £30
Gas, electric, water and sewerage:£180
Council tax: £110
TV licence: £12
Broadband: £40
Cleaning: £60
Total: £757
Profit: £1,433
(Note: This does not include agency management fees which can vary from 10–15% of gross rental cost.)

If you decide to refinance your project (and pull out money you have invested), the figures will change as you increase your borrowing costs. For the purpose of this example, let's assume that the revaluation of this property comes in at £180,000. The total cost of your project is £178,950. In order to extract *all* your money, you would need a valuation of £240,000. Unless properties in the area surrounding your HMO have also risen significantly in value, or you have bought at substantially below market value, it is unlikely you will be able to pull out all the cash you have initially invested.

If we assume a valuation of £180,000, you would be allowed 75% of that as a mortgage. – £135,000. This would leave you £43,950 in the deal.

£178, 950 – £135,000 = £43,950 (cost of project – remortgage amount)

Expenditure

Mortgage payment:£450 (new amount after revaluation)
Insurance: £30
Gas, electric, water and sewerage:£180
Council tax: £110
TV licence: £12
Broadband: £40
Cleaning: £60
Total: £757
Profit: £1,308

Returns

There are two ways to calculate the return on your investment

1. Return on investment (based on income divided by capital left in the project). Another way to put this is return on capital employed (ROCE):
2. Yield (based on income divided by total cost of the project)

Net income = £1,308 x 12 = £15,696
Capital left in = £43,950 ROI
(Capital left in /Net income)* 100= 35%
Net income/cost of project
= (15,696/178,950)* 100= 8% yield

I prefer to use the ROI or ROCE figure. This represents the

actual money that I have left in the deal (my money – or someone else's money). The rest is geared via a mortgage. If you use investor finance you can leverage the whole lot, but it's usual to start by using your own money as the seed capital. In which case, you can see that 35% return is an excellent return if you compare that with what you might get in a pension or a bank account. If you can pull all your money out of the deal, you will create an infinite return on your investment. The more deals you find like this, the more your money will work for you – so you don't have to work.

YIELDS AND CAPITAL GROWTH

Typically, when yields are high, capital growth is slower, a fact that is borne out by statistics across the UK property market. This is true in my investment area of south Cheshire and north Staffordshire. While we have seen some growth in line with general inflation, I can't say that capital growth over the last few years has been anything more than insipid. There is a benefit to that, however, which is that reinvestment becomes easier as values and prices are somewhat more predictable, and steadiness has its own benefits when building a property business. Wild fluctuations in values can destabilise future (and current) investment, as has been seen in the London property market. Huge variations in capital values over a few months makes it impossible to determine yields and return on investment accurately and creates the need for sound and multiple exit strategies.

Although a natural human reaction is to get excited when capital assets rise in value, ideally investing should be done with the head, not with the heart. Regular, dependable returns from property, compounding gradually over time is a core wealth-building strategy. HMOs fit very neatly into that bracket. If you desire large chunks of capital growth then perhaps this is not the strategy for you. Flips, developments, land acquisition and title splits might be better approaches. HMOs work well when the investor creates long-term cashflow and steady capital growth, where the property is not over-geared on revaluation, and where there is a good and increasing supply of tenants.

CREATING A PIPELINE OF DEALS

In order to create an ongoing pipeline of deals, having a sourcing process to follow will help you find a steady and regular supply of good deals. It is impossible to time these perfectly and you will often find that there's a dearth of good property deals for a few months, and then suddenly you get four in a week. Being prepared to react when you get a call is imperative, so that your potential vendor doesn't get cold feet about your unprepared reaction. Having a mindset that expects to see growth from the seeds you plant allows you to be aware and tuned into possibilities.

There are people everywhere having problems with their property. Either it needs too much work and they can't sell it, or they need to move abroad for work quickly, or they're getting divorced, or they're downsizing. These people often want a fast transaction and price is not the most important priority. Speed and certainty are their biggest concerns. They may have been thinking about putting the house up for sale in a traditional way with an estate agent, but have reservations about the process.

If you can find these sellers and know the ways you can offer a deal that works for you both, you create a real win-win.

There are plenty of places to find deals, and creating a sourcing pipeline needn't be difficult. You do need to be organised and have a structure in place to ensure that you maximise your chances of success. To find great properties and great deals you need four things:

1. Process
2. Perception
3. Paperwork
4. Persistence

Without a process you won't be able to create a steady stream of potential property deals. Without perception you could uncover a wealth of amazing properties but not know what to do with them. Without paperwork you can't finalise the deal. Without persistence you can't grow wealthy. As you can see, only two of these are practical actions – the other two are personal attributes. Finding deals needs you to be practical and personal.

1. Process

- Design a campaign. This gives your activity definition and purpose and allows you to learn each time from your mistakes and successes. I would recommend that you design a four-week campaign, in which you agree to target a particular area of no more than 1.5 square miles.
- Using a map, define the area you are going to target and find the postcodes that are part of this location. This will be the HMO location that you've already pinpointed.

Now locate all the shops, post offices, takeaways and supermarkets that serve that location.

- Next, you want to get some leaflets designed that tell people about you and how you can help them. (Please see Additional Resources section for recommendations of leaflet suppliers.) Some printers will provide ready-made templates ideal for leaflet campaigns of this type. You will want to repeat your campaign up to seven times before you see steady results. Order enough leaflets at the start to ensure you have enough volume to repeat your campaign regularly.
- Find a reputable leaflet delivery service. There are many ways you can achieve this – one is by working with a local takeaway service who are already delivering leaflets in the area. Another is by hiring independent leaflet distributors. Make sure you have a way of spot-testing the coverage of the drop.
- Write out a number of simple postcards that you can put up in shop windows locally. A suggested wording would be:

  'Struggling to sell your house? Do you need to move fast? I am looking for a house to buy and might be able to help you. Please get in touch to see if I can help you call Wendy on xxxxxxx.'

A simple postcard with a call to action is the best way to get your message across.

- The third aspect of your campaign is direct-to-landlord letters. You can download a sample letter from the website www.centreround.co.uk. The letter needs to be direct, friendly and polite. It needs to state what benefit you can offer to a landlord and how you can help them. One piece of advice: persistence is the key. I regularly receive letters from well-meaning investors who have found my details online and are offering to help me rent or sell my properties. I always wait until I've had a second letter before I respond. The sad thing is, I've rarely received that second letter. Remember that landlords who may be ready to sell want to know you are committed. One letter is not a sign of commitment.

- Another great tip is to incentivise your recipients in some way to meet with you. I mentored a female partnership who had no money to invest and were looking for a rent-to-rent deal to get started. I suggested that, to stand out from the crowd, in their letter they offered to meet up with the landlord and pay for a coffee. As a surprise incentive, even if the landlord was not willing to meet in person this time, I suggested that they include a voucher for a free coffee. As a result, they had a number of calls from investors, one that led to a profitable rent-to-rent deal making them over £800 profit per month. Be different.
- Your campaign should also include contacting all the people like estate agents that you've already started to engage with, and should include networking like crazy.
- Plan your diary so that you can give yourself deadlines and structure. You don't need to complete all your actions in week one.
- After you've completed the four weeks, spend some time analysing what went well and what didn't. It takes time and experience to execute a great campaign. Now you need to wait for your seeds to flourish – plan the next campaign and followup any leads you have generated.

2. Perception

Perception gives you insight into the possible motivations of a seller so that you can delve into the real reasons for a fast and efficient sale. This is a vital skill as it means you can cut to the chase and start negotiating on terms that are meaningful to you both. Perceiving what will work is a core skill when negotiating with people and, if you rush into the details of an offer too quickly, you may miss important details.

Educating yourself about the various strategies available to secure property is also a must. Without education I would have overlooked many potential deals that crossed my desk. It's by understanding what makes a deal work that you will be ahead of the crowd, and you'll be able to work with vendors, agents, local people and your contacts with confidence and insight. Knowing how to adopt the right strategies in particular situations, coupled with understanding people, will allow you to find and negotiate great deals.

Knowing the different approaches for securing property deals will allow you to have a number of strategies to use in addition to the usual route of traditional buying. This will give you confidence to negotiate deals. It will also bring you a streak of creativity when it comes to funding. Many sellers are not necessarily looking for cash. Although their property is up for sale, and it apparently looks as if a purchase transaction is what's required, many vendors have reasons they *have* to dispose of the property even though selling is the least beneficial to them. They don't know what you know and therefore choose to go to an estate agent to sell the house. They simply don't realise that other strategies are possible. It's your job to work with them and use your knowledge to help them too.

Other vendors are desperate to sell and need a fast transaction. So, in an environment where sellers want *speed* and *certainty*, how can you work with that? Unless you understand the process for executing a deal fast, you won't be able to meet the needs of a seller and you will most likely lose out on a possible deal.

In the negotiation for a deal, then, perception and awareness is key. If you struggle with this, here are some tips to help you:

- Put the vendor first. Make sure you listen more than you talk and hear more than you speak.
- Create rapport by asking pertinent and meaningful questions. Watch the person to see how they react to you, and whether they are nervous, shy or wary. Are they a dominant person, a decisive person or an impatient person? Take some time to find out a bit about them but be aware of their motivation. Don't prod too far immediately or spend too long on meaningless chatter. There is a maxim in psychology which is 'pace, pace, pace, lead'. In other words, let the other person set the pace while you set the structure. Then you can mould the interaction and lead the discussion.
- Have a list of questions already prepared, but sense when it's time to stop. There are facts you'll need to gather to assess whether you can form a deal or not. Some people want to get to the point of the offer immediately and others are assessing you to see if they even want to do a deal. Don't rush into making an offer or saying something you'll later regret. If you sense that the other person wants to rush you (which is common if they're motivated to sell) just explain – 'So that I can make you the best offer, I just need to go away and crunch the numbers. I'm sure you'd rather I got this

right than messed you around?'. Most people will say yes to that.

- After any interaction with someone spend some time reflecting on what you learnt. What did you observe? What were the give-away clues about the motivation of the vendor? What conclusions could you draw about whether a deal is possible on a personal basis? Did you rush the discussion? How were you feeling throughout?
- It is impossible to predict the outcome of a discussion at this point. Stay calm and positive and press on with your next steps.

3. Paperwork

Having the right structure to do the deal once you've found a motivated vendor is vital. Before starting any paperwork, you need to gather some core pieces of information from a vendor (seller). These pieces of information are best gathered face to face. Your leaflets and postcards and letters will generate interest and phonecalls. You need to be prepared to take some basic information on the phone. However, the idea is that by meeting in person you can create far more rapport and trust and have a much greater chance of creating a deal that will work for you both.

Without the following pieces of information, you won't be able to come up with a succinct, clear and precise plan that benefits you both. The core pieces of information to gather are:

- Address and details of the property and the vendor
- How long the vendor has owned the house/property
- How quickly the vendor needs to/wants to sell
- What the reasons for the sale are (divorce, downsizing, moving abroad, paying off debt etc.)

- Why the property isn't up for sale already with an estate agent
- Are other people to be involved in the decision (partner, parent, siblings etc.)?
- Is there any debt on the property (mortgage, second charge, bridging finance)?
- If there's a mortgage, how much is it, what type is it and what's the remaining term
- Has a purchase of another property already been agreed?
- Would the vendor be prepared to let out the property rather than sell it?
- Has the vendor got plans for the money from the sale?

Once you have these core pieces of information you can then go away and crunch your numbers and come up with a suitable offer. There might be a number of different possibilities, so be sure to present them clearly and slowly. Chances are your vendor has never heard of some of them and was awaiting a simple purchase price offer. Practice your delivery with someone who can give you fair feedback if you are unsure of your ability to be clear.

Once you've had a successful meeting, you've come up with a plan, and an agreed way to proceed, it is vital that this is captured in a heads of terms agreement. This simply lays out the roles and responsibilities that the partners in the agreement will take. This needs to be signed and each partner should have a copy. The heads of terms agreement then forms the basis for your legal documentation. I always advise people to take legal advice on any deal. However, it's worth bearing in mind that many general property solicitors are not well-versed in creative deal strategies. You may have to refer your specialists to your vendor in order for the deal to proceed.

4. Persistence

Sourcing an attractive deal takes patience and determination. It takes time to set up the pipeline and time to negotiate with the vendor. It may take a few weeks before you see results from your persistence. You may get a few phone calls that lead nowhere. You may feel like you're wasting your time and money. However, in property, like investing generally, persistence pays off. Don't let your early failures or lack of progress set you back.

After a number of months being seen and heard in our local area, telling people what we were doing and what I was looking for, I hadn't seen much progress. I began to wonder whether it was worth all the effort and time I was putting in. I was sitting at my desk one day when I received a phone call from a man who didn't want to pay for an estate agent to sell his house. The house was a great size and in a good location for an HMO. I was first in the queue. By being known in my local area, I had a distinct advantage when it came to buying or negotiating a deal. He and his wife wanted to downsize, having raised their family in this spacious terraced property. However, the house needed some work to make it attractive to a family buyer – cash he didn't have. I was able to sit down with him and work out exactly what he needed to move on and how we could benefit too by creating a win-win solution that worked for us both. He was delighted to save the money that otherwise he would have spent with an agent, leaving him more to put towards a smaller house. In this situation, knowing the strategies that can be used in property deals is paramount, as a simple purchase transaction is only one of many that can be employed to buy and secure property.

Remember Edison's famous words when you're tired and feel like you're getting nowhere, and when you've had little results from your efforts:

'Our greatest weakness lies in giving up. The most certain way to succeed is always to try just one more time'
—Thomas Edison

CASE STUDY

I was driving past one of our mini-HMOs (a three-bed HMO) when I saw an identical property a few doors away up for sale. I checked online and it was available at £85,000. I knew this was a reasonable price as we had recently had our mini-mo revalued at £100,000. So, I booked a viewing with the agent and met the owner at the property. It was immediately apparent why this house hadn't sold: it was riddled with damp, condensation and mould. The vendor had a massive problem though – she had agreed a sale on her house a few weeks before which had fallen through and, in her haste, had put down a £20,000 deposit on a brand new house. If she didn't move into the new house within the next month, she would lose the new house and her deposit.

I could see she needed a fast sale, so I called my solicitor and asked him what the fastest transaction time possible could be – he said a fortnight. So, I put in an offer: £72,000.

The vendor was highly relieved to receive the offer, but I knew that the cost of the repairs would be high. She accepted the offer on the proviso that we complete by her deadline. I insisted on a specialist damp and timber report, which showed the cost of works to be over £10,000. I had to revise the offer due to the substantial costs involved. So, I went back and offered £60,000. By now, the vendor was getting frantic. She was worried she would lose her new house and was calling me daily to assess progress.

This is where your tenacity starts to be tested. I didn't want to fleece this lady, but I knew that I was her last hope. I also knew that without getting the house at the right price, we couldn't do a deal. She would lose her beautiful brand-new home and I would potentially lose a deal. The balance in creating a solution that both parties are happy with is never easy to achieve. The offer was rejected – so I increased it to £61,500 to pay for her estate agency fees. I felt that if I could help her a little further, then we could both get what we wanted. I was delighted when she said yes and accepted the revised price. We completed within her timeframe so she could move into her brand-new house and, on her moving day, I sent her a large bouquet of flowers to thank her. She was overjoyed with the result. A real win-win was achieved.

FINDING THE RIGHT TENANT TYPE

Whilst the focus of our business and to a large extent this book, is on working professional tenants, there are other tenant types you may wish to create HMOs for such as

- Students
- Older people

- Foreign friendship groups
- Short-term lets (bridging HMOs and Serviced Accommodation)
- LHA (Local Housing Authority)
- Social care

Each group has its pros and cons, but the key to making a business work is to know the market you're focusing on. How much do you know your buyer? What kind of accommodation will suit their needs best? Do they want to pay higher rents in return for better services? Or is budget the main concern for them, in which case they're prepared to compromise on luxury? Do they need access to superfast broadband (who doesn't these days?!), and are en-suites a necessity to attract the right tenants for your business? Will the type of tenant you rent to affect other aspects of your business such as mortgages and insurance?

Finding out the needs of your market before entering that market will prepare you for the unexpected and ensure that you set up your HMO suitably from the start. If you've never undertaken market research before, now is a good time. Rather than assessing the competition in your area, assess your market – your potential customers. Before investing in HMOs I spoke to tens of tenants – on Facebook, in the street, in shops locally. I wanted to understand what made them tick and what they were looking for in an ideal houseshare. It was eye-opening. Many of them said that the mix of tenants in the house was the most important aspect to them of sharing a house. Not en-suites, not fabulous decor, not even price. Regular research in the rental market is undertaken by various agencies, one of which demonstrated that pricing was a deeply sensitive criteria for tenants.[8]

Understanding your market is core to a good business – and HMOs are no exception. This is an area about which I am constantly learning. It fascinates me to know how people live, what suits their needs and what their preferences are. If you can adopt an enquiring mind about what other people want, and a belief that you can help others by providing it, you'll gain clarity immediately on how to *find it*.

ACTION STATION

The key to finding the right property is

- Finding the Right Area
- Finding the Right Property
- Finding the Right Deal
- Finding the Right Tenant Type

What do you need to do now to ensure you have all these four bases covered? Which of these do you need to get out and get covered first? Don't get into analysis paralysis. Make a decision to research two areas. Compare and contrast your numbers. Walk the streets, talk to people. Become an expert in your area. Know the local geography and where the bus stops and cafes are. Don't be scared to make mistakes – look silly and learn. Learning this is what will make you money.

8 Knight Frank, 2012.

CHAPTER 7

FUND IT

'There's no shortage of money in this world: start hustling'
—Grant Cordone

When you understand the way money works, over and above the practicalities of managing it, you will be able to utilise far more of it than you currently have access to. Even if you're starting with a healthy amount of cash, continuing to source and buy property will mean that, sooner or later, your initial seed capital will run out. If your goal is to create ongoing residual income, you'll need to make sure you either have access to funds yourself, or access to other people's money. Understanding how to construct deals creatively and legally with no money, *and* being able to raise money from investors, will continue to catapult your progress. Although many people are scared and wary of using other people's money, you'll find it to be an absolute necessity if you don't have much of your own money to start with or you're investing in an area where property prices are more than £1,500 per square metre.

In this chapter you'll learn various strategies for using money wisely for investing in HMOs. Whether using traditional mortgages and bank loans, or securing deals using creative strategies and other people's money, funding your portfolio is all about using money as a resource to create your dreams.

BUYING AN HMO

An ordinary purchase transaction works as follows:

- You identify the property you want to buy;
- You agree on a price with the vendor (often using an estate agent to liaise between you);
- You both initiate a transaction by commissioning your solicitors to undertake the conveyancing;
- If you need a mortgage, you'll work with a mortgage broker to identify the right 'product' (mortgage);
- Once the contract is agreed and signed, it will be exchanged and a date for completion will be set. (These two aspects may be completed on the same day.);
- On the day of completion, you will legally have the title and deeds of the property transferred into your possession, along with any charges that are levied by the mortgage company for the debt that you now owe for the purchase;
- Practical issues are dealt with, then keys are handed over to you and the property is yours.

Although this process is by far the most common way to transact property in the UK, there are many other methods that allow you to secure property without having a mortgage, which were briefly discussed in the last chapter. The majority of HMOs are bought using the traditional method of conveyancing and I would recommend that you develop a power team to help you as this will probably be the way you will build your initial portfolio.

At the start, the people you need in your power team are:

- Solicitor with a conveyancing specialism
- Mortgage broker
- Bookkeeper
- Accountant
- Builder
- Insurance broker

At this point you need people who will save you time and money undertaking specialist roles that you cannot do. You may also wish to use the services of a property sourcer – someone who finds deals for you. Financially you need to be prepared for a number of costs even at the initial stage of purchase. These are:

- Deposit (unless you are buying the property without a mortgage)*or*
- Cash for the full amount of the purchase price
- Stamp duty
- Legal costs
- Mortgage arrangement fee
- Surveyor's fee

BUYING STRUCTURE

In the past, buying property was most often done personally, in your own name. However, with the drastic changes to income tax from residential property, if you want to create a handful of properties that bring you steady residual income, I would recommend that you set up a limited company in which to invest.

There are more mortgage products now available to HMO investors and a limited company structure gives you flexibility about how and when you draw out the profits of the company. If you make a personal loan into the company as seed funding for investment, you can withdraw this tax-free once you have finished and refinanced the first project – thus enabling you to create a steady income stream initially free of tax. You will need to have annual accounts produced and ensure sound administration of running a limited company. With a good property accountant and online bookkeeping tools like Xero, QuickBooks or Quickfile this is not a daunting prospect. You are creating a business with inherent value, so it's worth structuring this correctly from the start.

Organise your money and affairs before you start to move money around. Having your money organised into a different bank account for your business from the beginning will help you when it comes to tracking your finances. Money management means getting organised from the start. Laying good foundations will make it much easier in the long run to manage and account for your business finances. There's nothing worse than having four or five properties and not knowing exactly how much money they are making you and how much money you can save by doing things differently. Tracking your cashflow and your profit and loss figures should be a basic activity that you instil from day one of owning your first investment property. This is of course where a good bookkeeper (or online system that you run yourself) comes in. Here are a few other tips to ensure you are mortgage-ready:

- Check your credit score regularly and ensure your credit file is accurate and up to date using the services of an online credit file service such as Experian or Equifax.

- Make sure you are on the electoral register.
- Pay all of your bills on time.
- Pay off high levels of consumer debt first (anything over 12% APR).
- Transfer all high APR credit to 0% interest rates or as close to as possible. (If you are in serious debt speak to a debt counselling service or a mortgage broker to create a plan to reduce this before you start applying for mortgages.)
- Don't apply for credit in dribs and drabs. It's better to apply all on day one so that your file is not 'dinged' repeatedly.
- If you are using a limited company through which to invest, set up a limited company business bank account to track all outgoings and income
- If you do decide to invest using a limited company there will be other costs such as a personal guarantee for the mortgage to bear in mind.

Other information you'll need:

- P60 or SA302 from your tax return
- Your last three months' bank statements
- Your last three months' payslips
- Proof of bonuses/commission
- Your latest P60 tax form (showing income and tax paid from each tax year)
- Your last three years' accounts or tax returns
- Proof of deposits (e.g., savings account statements)
- ID documents (usually a passport)
- Proof of address (e.g., utility bills or credit card bills)

CASE STUDY

After buying a few houses that I had turned into HMOs, I'd built up a good relationship with a lot of the local estate agents in our area, which is why it's always important to get out there building relationships from the start. I was starting to get some proactive calls from agents, who phoned me when they thought they had a property that we might be interested in as an HMO. One day I received a call from a local agent called Carol who asked me if I would be interested in viewing a house that they had just taken on as a 'corporate sale' (this is estate agent speak for a repossession). She told me the address of the house and I was immediately interested because we already had a very successful HMO just a few doors away. She told me that the property had literally just been listed and wanted to organise viewings as soon as possible. I agreed to meet her that afternoon and carry out a viewing at the house.

We met at the property and immediately I knew that this house would be ideal as an HMO. The rooms were a good size, the kitchen was light, long and bright and I could see this house being a fantastic five-bed all en-suite HMO. There were a couple of cracks in the walls but not big enough to worry me. So I put in an offer. The 'corporate' had put the house up at £85,000, so I offered the full asking price to take it off the market. Carol was delighted and said that once she'd returned to the office she would immediately get back to me.

Later that afternoon, she called me to say 'Sorry, Wendy, we've had a higher offer'. I was disappointed but raised my bid by another £2,000. Again, the same response: 'Sorry, Wendy, you've been outbid again'. I thought the best way was to set a highest limit on my price as I didn't want to get into an out-of-auction bidding war. 'Carol, my top price is £93,000', (decided purely as this was the price I'd paid for my other property a few doors down).A day later I received a call back from her with bad news: 'I'm afraid Wendy you've lost the sale. The other party outbid you.' 'Ok, Carol, thank you. Please let me know how it goes.'

A couple of weeks later, the phone rang again and it was Carol. 'Wendy, the house sale on Gainsborough Road has just fallen through, and I wondered if you might be interested in starting from scratch again with an offer?'

'Carol, can you tell me why the previous sale fell through please?'

'The survey from the mortgage company came back saying the property had structural problems', she said

'Would you mind if I asked my structural engineer to take a look then before we make an offer'? I asked.

'No, that's fine', she said.

That afternoon I called our structural engineer and explained the problem to him. I asked him to attend the property and carry out a structural survey and report back to me his findings. At this point we had no offer accepted so it was a risk. I could pay for the survey only to find that someone else had stepped in front of me in the queue and made an acceptable offer. I knew too, however, that if there were structural problems, the only buyers could be cash buyers, so we were in with a strong chance of success *if* we could find the answer to the structural deficit. I was prepared to take the chance and pay the structural engineer's fee of £350. Sometimes you have to put some skin in the game and take a risk. You have to spend money to make money.

Within a few days the structural engineer had come back to me.

'Wendy, I'm about to send the report but I thought you should know that basically the house is sound. The only two things that need attention are the tree roots of the tree at the front of the house and the RSJ [reinforced steel joist] which is not big enough in the kitchen extension to support it fully. It should have been bigger when the extension was carried out. If you remediate these two things, you'll be fine.'

I called Carol immediately.

'Carol', I said, 'it's not good news' (with sucking in of teeth). 'The structural engineer's report is back and there are some expensive changes we'll need to include. I'm really sorry, but the most I can possibly offer at this point is £80,000.'

'Thanks, Wendy', she said. 'Let me see what I can do.'

Ten minutes later the phone rang and it was Carol.

'Good news, Wendy. The offer's been accepted. You've got it for £80,000.'

The only problem was that I didn't have the money to buy it. My money had run out many months before.

I remembered the quote I had heard about success being

where preparation and opportunity meet. I wondered who I should call. Immediately I phoned my investor. He was a man I'd met at a networking meeting who was running another business and wanted to invest in HMOs. After running the numbers past him and giving him the background to my other HMO on the same street, he was delighted with this opportunity. He offered to put all the money in and we would go 50/50 on the return. We already had a limited company set up that gave us each 50% of the shares in the company, so the structure was in place. Within just a few weeks, the house was teaming with tradesmen and the refurb was happening.

We turned that property into a five-bed all-en-suite HMO. I used none of my own money and it currently makes between £900–1,150 profit per month. It revalued at £155,000 after a build cost of £53,000 thus allowing us to refinance and leave just £17k in the deal. The ROI is 70%.

As there was money left in the deal, I agreed with my investor to share in 50% of that (£8.5k) and to add it back into the company, thus maintaining our 50% balance and continuing to take 50% of profits – a great arrangement that works to this day. I learnt that when you find a great deal, you need to have already built up a relationship with an investor. I had foreseen that without the right structure and arrangement in place, there was no way I could have taken the risk of putting in spurious offers and keeping my fingers crossed that I would find the money. In property, you have to have two pipelines you're constantly working on – a deals pipeline and a funding pipeline. In this case it was the confidence to act swiftly and smartly that allowed us to get it at a good price and make it into a wonderful HMO.

RAISING FINANCE FOR AN HMO

Knowing the rules of property will help you negotiate deals. Knowing the rules of money will help you raise finance.

One of the most important skills that you can learn to accelerate your growth is that of raising money from other people: Using Other People's Money or OPM as it is sometimes called. This is the magic bullet of investing. Using OPM is crucial to continued investing. Once you learn how to find a deal and present a deal to an investor, your ability to secure five HMOs will be easy. It may feel scary at first. This is completely normal. It's very likely that you will be nervous about your credibility, experience and ability to create a return for your investor. This is one of the reasons why many people never get far with property. They are unwilling to take get out of their comfort zone to practise life-long core skills such as raising finance, selling themselves, and being able to pitch a deal. Ultimately, it's your choice whether you use OPM or not. All I can tell you is that using OPM is the difference between ticking over and taking off. I can assure you that if you continue to invest in property, you will run out of your own money at some point. Your appetite for property investing will increase as you gain momentum, but without the right support, and the right financial resources to fuel the increase, you will become stuck.

TYPES OF INVESTOR

Before you start running around asking people for money, here are a few tips to help you raise money credibly, legitimately and strategically. When you start to use money from investors, you need to be aware of your legal responsibilities.(The Financial Conduct Authority has rules around investments, which I would suggest you read – FCA PS13/03 is the guidance.) Just as there are many different types of people in the world, there are different types of investor. You will no doubt meet many people on your investing journey and this list of 'investor types' is not exhaustive.

The definition of an investor, according to *The Cambridge Dictionary*, is 'a person who puts money into something in order to make a profit or get an advantage'.[9] Determining exactly what the profit or advantage the investor will gain will be part of the pitch you make to raise the money.

The FCA rules also stipulate the arrangements you can legitimately create, based on the financial wherewithal of the investor – namely whether they are a 'retail', 'high net worth' or 'sophisticated' investor. Ideally, you want a good match between your project or development and the type of investor. If the two don't match up you may find you have some difficulties along the way. Your investor might be happy to lend you money for a year, but want it back for another project in 12 months' time. That person is concerned about return of cash plus the interest gained. Another person may be more interested in long-term gains and want security in the property itself. Each person, each project, each partnership has its own risks and returns.

Knowing the various structures you can use will help you approach investors wisely, understand their needs and apply that to the project you need funding. I would always recommend that you take professional legal and financial advice when you

9 *The Cambridge Dictionary*, 2015.

are getting into partnership with other people. Ensure you are meeting FCA regulations about the level of money and experience your investor has, and their prior relationship to you, before you begin to pitch a deal.

1. Cash investor. This is someone who has got money to invest, which is currently sitting in a bank or in stocks and shares. The returns could be quite low and the investor is not happy about the returns they're getting. They just want money in money out. You can find many cash investors with as much as £200k sitting in low interest accounts. They may be fairly risk-averse and not inclined to personally get involved in property investing. However, they might be delighted to receive a much better return by lending you the money. In this case, they are willing to lend you a short-term cash investment, which can be anything from tens to hundreds of thousands of pounds. The bottom line for them is what *return* they are getting. Ensure you get the paperwork correct by giving them a contract for the loan and a schedule of repayment. You cannot borrow money from a private investor to put into your limited company for property investment unless you are FCA regulated, so a loan such as this has to be a person-to-person loan. Therefore, for any sum larger than £30,000 I would suggest you also produce a personal guarantee and some form of external security to guarantee the repayment of the money.
2. The second type of investor is the investor who wants to pay you for your services. This is more of a transactional relationship; where they will pay you for sourcing and project management and they will incentivise you for tenanting and other additional services. You might offer a whole suite of services to a transactional investor. This

investor is looking for *results*. In this situation, you'll need a contract that details the services you'll provide, with an agreed payment plan. As this is a transactional relationship, payment terms and conditions will support this investment running smoothly. Don't just rely on a few email exchanges to be sufficient as a form of contract. You need to create and produce comprehensive terms to clarify the responsibilities of each party.

3. The third type of investor is a person who wants to develop a portfolio in a partnership structure. This person is ideal for a joint venture (JV).They may have quite a lot of capital to invest and may already be busy in their own business or job. Their motivation is to save time by using your knowledge and skills, and in return to act as the financier. These investors are looking for more long-term asset building portfolio services which give them a *relationship*. It's likely that you will want to establish a limited company as your working structure so you each share in the ownership and income. Your shareholding does not have to be 50/50, although this is usual. I would recommend that you draw up a partnership agreement detailing the roles and responsibilities of the partners in conjunction with the percentage split. This will sit alongside the company's memorandum and articles, which are legal requirements when setting up a limited company.
4. The fourth type of investor is the one-off joint venture project partner. This investor is not ready or not willing to commit to a long-term partnership. They are looking for a larger project such as a development or a large refurb such as a commercial conversion. They may have a view to doing more in future but initially they want to

create a special purpose vehicle (SPV) to enable one project to be completed. This investor is mostly looking for *reward*.

A blend of the JV paperwork and a contract will be needed for an investment of this kind. In fact, once you start to raise money from more experienced investors, it is likely you will have far more requirements to meet in terms of project planning, risk and return analysis.

Each of these investor types has differing preferences and requirements. Understanding an investor first is fundamental to whether the project will be the right one for their money. Having said that, the way you work is also crucial to the survival of the relationship. Many investors start by investing small and testing out the process and the relationship. This is a tried and tested risk-protection strategy. However, many investors have more money to invest than they later reveal.

It would be easy to feel overwhelmed and lost at the idea of using OPM. This is where having advice and guidance from a mentor can be especially valuable – especially as you may lack confidence and belief in your ability to raise money. Remember that building a relationship with an investor often takes time and requires persistence.

I like to imagine the relationship like a series of double doors intersecting a long hotel corridor. Each double door represents the next step in the relationship. The entrance of the corridor is the lobby and represents your initial introduction to your investor. The end of the corridor is where the safe is kept and represents the exchange of money from your investor to you.

In between are a series of double doors to go through, lounges to contemplate life and lifts to get off. Staying patient, understanding the rules of play, and imagining this sequence will support you in never running out of investment funds again.

TESTIMONIAL

'I attended Wendy's weekend HMO course as a young entrepreneur owning a virtual assistant company with the view of assisting my dad and wife further in their property business… but I felt so empowered by Wendy, I realised I had the drive to start my own journey in property.

I had no intention of becoming an investor myself. With three young children, and a husband who regularly works away, I thought that there was no way I could buy an HMO (and anyway I didn't have any money). The weekend course was so inspirational and informative that I began to wonder if I could create residual income from investing in HMOs myself. Within a few days of getting home from the course I decided to join Wendy's mentoring programme. I'd seen a perfect house online which met all of Wendy's criteria for an HMO. It was on by the "Modern Method of Auction" which basically meant it was an estate agent selling it at a reduced price for a fast sale. The fees were £6,000. I spoke to Wendy about it and we went through my numbers. She was encouraging and so I put in an offer, which was accepted. I paid the fee… on my credit card!

My problem was, I didn't have the money to buy it, or

to do the refurb!

With Wendy's help, I put a pitch together for an investor, and I couldn't believe it when I had the money from him in my bank account a few weeks later! He could see what I was trying to achieve and was willing to support me and invest in the project. Within six months I had my first luxury five-bed HMO up and running!

Wendy has been very supportive and encouraging with my new business and has guided me with lots of decision making, systems and process and business development. The mentoring programme has given me the one-to-one support I have required and also the opportunity to meet lots of people on the same property journey and has even resulted in finding someone else to work with.

Thank you, Wendy, for making me believe in myself and making all this possible, I couldn't have done it without you!'

Charlotte Firth

WORKING WITH INVESTORS

There are four areas to consider when you start to work with investors:

1. Commitment
2. Communication
3. Clear purpose of project

4. Clarity of entry and exit

Your **commitment** to developing a portfolio of properties (even just five) starts with your own honesty. Are you ready to walk this path, with all the ensuing struggles, skirmishes and strife? Developing property can be hard work in the early days. You need to be sure this is what you want and that you are committed to it. A savvy investor can see through someone who is not committed and won't want to throw money at a person who cannot demonstrate obvious and sustained commitment.

Communication is a visible sign of commitment. Create a communication plan that outlines when and how you will communicate with your investor. This will depend partly on the relationship and what stage it's at. If your investor is very keen and has the money ready, then a regular call with an agenda and clear outputs will be appropriate. However, whilst kindling this relationship, you should adopt a more relaxed approach, until you get a clear steer that the investor would like to see a potential pitch for a project.

Having a **clear purpose** for a project will enable you to legitimately pitch it to an investor, as you will already know what is their preferred investment strategy. Will this be a long-term investment? Are you looking for short-term loan funding? If you have the vision for a portfolio of property, can the investor also commit to a handful of properties at this stage? What kinds of returns are likely to be achieved with regard to yields, income, capital growth? Can you demonstrate your knowledge about this type of project if you haven't already? What would be suitable criteria and what would fall foul of being acceptable?

Clarity of entry and exit. Without this you won't be able to describe the points at which funding will be needed. You may decide to mix an investor's funds with a mortgage so that you can finance the purchase and the refurb. There may be project dates when extra funding will be needed, or when there are decisions to be made that will need a further drawdown. Clarity about when the money will be required, how much will the investor gain by being involved in the project and what the exit will be for the finances all need to be thought through and planned from the start. It's often best to suggest a couple of options at the start and see which ones 'float the boat' of your investor. From your initial discussions, you'll figure out what kind of investor they are and create a plan accordingly.

One of the key issues that you'll face will be clarity of exit. For many people this question really means 'how can I get all my money out of the project?' By refinancing your project after the refurb is complete and filling the house with tenants to demonstrate an income stream, you can present the property to a mortgage company for a revaluation.

ADDING VALUE TO AN HMO

You may have been educated to realise that the momentum of releasing money from one deal to use as capital for the next creates momentum for effective wealth-building. It is one of the best ways to grow a portfolio, recycling money each and every time you finish a project. Doing this five times is all you need to create life-changing income. It's really as simple as that. However, changes to the marketplace, regulation and government attitudes towards investors means it is becoming increasingly difficult for investors to extract all their money out of HMO developments, especially if they are new to the market. Many lenders have tightened their criteria so that there is some 'skin left in the game' by the investor after the development has been completed –meaning that no matter what you do, you will *not* be able to recycle all your cash when you refinance after the development is completed. So, what can you do to avoid getting stuck with capital left in a project? And how can you best insure yourself against that happening?

Having bought, sold and refurbished nearly 35 properties worth over £6m, we have plenty of experience of developing properties that have valued up, thus allowing all the money to be pulled out of the development. We have also had some developments where we have left money in the deal. I wouldn't necessarily say that the latter were 'worse deals' than the former. There are ways to assess and evaluate a project, which consider more than just whether you have pulled all your money out. However, there are a few key areas that when actioned can create a far better chance of getting all your money out.

You make money when you buy, not when you sell. It's an adage that seems rather counter-intuitive, but it's absolutely true. Buying a property at the right price is a fundamental first step to adding value. When you buy below market value, you immediately lock in value as, compared to other properties of a similar size, age and state, you are already making money by buying below market value. Relying on capital gains is not a sound strategy for HMOs because house prices can be volatile. There are clever ways to find properties below market value but they all depend on finding a buyer who is motivated.

We once bought a single buy-to-let at a considerably reduced price (about 24% below market value) because the tenant had moved out of the house and the landlord had no cash to bring it up to a standard whereby it would re-rent. He therefore had to sell. After we had carried out some basic renovations costing roughly £6k (new kitchen and decoration plus carpets throughout), the house was valued at over £32k more than we had paid for it, allowing us to remortgage and pull all our money out.

During the conveyancing process on another property that we bought for development as an HMO, we discovered that the garden was hiding Japanese Knotweed. We had a full survey, which estimated the cost of complete removal and destruction of the knotweed, plus remedial work on the garden, to be in the thousands of pounds. By taking this figure back to the vendor we reduced the price of the house accordingly. Once the work was completed and insured (*very important if you are removing JKW*) we were easily able to refinance the HMO on a commercial basis. If you can find problems with properties, you will find deals. If you can find motivated sellers, you can find deals. If you become a problem solver rather than a problem creator, you will find *lots* of deals and this is still the first and the best strategy for creating long-term value.

Substantially alter the layout. This is a second approach, which relies on heavy capital investment and thus is not always possible for investors who are starting out on their HMO investment journey. I'm referring here to putting en-suites in all of the rooms, perhaps even small kitchenettes, moving walls and reconfiguring the layout so that the property is clearly only for use as an HMO and without serious work will never be used as a family house again. Getting good plans drawn up by a technically competent person (such as an architectural technician) will also allow you to explore other creative options for a property that a trained eye can spot. There is a risk that 'units' that are more substantial than bedrooms can incur separate council tax bandings and therefore bills. Do your local research to understand if this is likely to happen before you go ahead.

Extend the property. As is the case in standard residential properties, adding extra space to a house can add significant value when designed and executed well. You could add a loft extension, cellar room, or a rear extension to the property, all increasing the rental yield of the house and adding valuable space. Additional areas that are already attached to buildings such as garages, workshops or conservatory lean-tos can also be used for conversion (subject to getting the necessary consents). The use of redundant but pre-established space on the footprint of a property has been a well-used hack that developers have historically used to add many thousands of pounds of income to an HMO property. Some of our best performing HMOs are ones we have bought with additional space such as this and converted into additional living or bedroom areas.

Great design. Creating beautiful, contemporary and exceptional spaces in which tenants can live is an aspiration for many HMO investors. There are many inspirational ideas you can apply to do this without spending the earth. Lighting, colour, clever use of space, creative touches and unique details can all create a 'wow' factor in an HMO, which even valuers are impressed by. Minor improvements such as bathrooms and kitchens of course also improve the look and feel of an HMO. However, in terms of assuring cash out of the deal, this approach is more tricky and may require you to combine this with one of the other approaches I've outlined above to maximise the impact that good interior design can have. We developed a small 'mini-mo' in Stoke-on-Trent, which was bought below market value at £61,000. We spent £26,000 on the refurb, which was a huge amount of money compared to its value. However, the property valued up at £100,000 on a bricks and mortar basis. We left just £2k in the deal and it nets us a profit of £550 per month – this for a small three-bed house. The valuer was delighted when he turned up and said it was one of the best-looking properties he had ever seen in Stoke.

REFINANCING AN HMO

Refinancing can be a minefield if you don't know what you're doing and if you don't have a good broker. Having a good broker can be the difference between being able to accelerate your growth with HMOs and grinding to a halt. Your mortgage broker should be efficient, fast and an excellent communicator. You need to find someone who will represent you to lenders and who understands you and your business.

Using an experienced and well-connected mortgage broker is crucial to get the best valuation on a property. Without experience and specialist knowledge of the marketplace you may end up with an offer and a valuation that does not fully reflect the value you've created. By working closely with your mortgage broker, they will fully understand your business, your personal situation and agree an approach to risk (again often not discussed but vital when it comes to deciding on your HMO borrowing strategy). Some lenders are happy to value on a full commercial basis (i.e. on a net income multiplier). Others are more cautious and prefer what I call a 'hybrid' valuation approach – a mid-way figure that sits roughly half-way between bricks and mortar and commercial.

Each lender has their own policy guidance that they use to advise valuers on their panel. While this is not something you can easily influence, you can reject a valuation of a property if you feel it is not reflective of the value you have created. If you are buying with a mortgage and then plan to refinance after the development is completed, a good plan to make this strategy work will ensure you meet all the lender's requirements before and afterwards (especially if there is a possibility of refinancing onto a new HMO mortgage product with a different lender).

For example, Precise mortgage's requirements include:

1. Experience: experienced landlords only. Applicants must have held a current buy-to-let for at least 12 months prior to application. No first-time landlords;
2. Occupancy: properties with up to eight bedrooms accepted;
3. Minimum valuation: £250k in London, £100k elsewhere;
4. Rental cover –interest cover ratio: bespoke ICRs based on individual circumstances to help you to maximise the loan size.[10]

If you don't meet these requirements you won't be able to access this mortgage product. Another option is a bridge to term product that allows you to buy, develop and then refinance with an end valuation in mind. Although this is not completely reliable as a determined end value, it will give you

10 Taken from http://www.precisemortgages.co.uk/BuyToLet/HMOLimitedCompany accessed 23 March 2018.

some comfort as to a potential figure. As they say, forewarned is forearmed.

Your mortgage broker should also help you evaluate the best type of mortgage for your needs. Do you really want a commercial revaluation to pull out all your money? In some areas, it would be preferable *not* to get a commercial valuation if the bricks and mortar value of the property is higher than the commercial multiplier of net rents. Also, you must consider the impact on your cashflow if you gear your portfolio highly. By increasing the value of a property, you may be able to pull out all your seed capital – but does it make sense to do it? If the mortgage payments result in creating a risk for your business if your HMO is not fully occupied 100% of the time, is it really right to take out all your money? If you do get a valuation that allows you to withdraw all the added value you have created, what is your plan for the money? Having a good accountant and tax specialist at this stage will be vital so that you maximise the positive result you have created. Your age, attitude to risk and overall strategy will help determine the answers to these questions.

EXIT STRATEGY

It may seem completely at odds of building a business to be thinking about the end just as you begin to build your HMO portfolio but as Cicero, the Roman philosopher, once said 'Before beginning plan carefully'. Considering your exit strategy early on in the process allows you to consider options that you might not otherwise have thought of, such as the implication for inheritance tax when you pass on your portfolio or when you die; the implications of your partnership should your JV partner wish to liquidate their part of the ownership of your portfolio. Or it might simply be that you don't want to end up in 20 years' time with properties where you still owe the majority of the capital. Now is the time to consider your intended exit strategy (even if that changes over the course of the time you are investing).

Your vision will determine your path. Your exit strategy is a gate along the way.

Many people will advise you to think of your exit strategy as part of the project evaluation process. It's often when we slow down and stand back to consider the future that we start to contemplate what will happen to our assets when we are no longer here. You may have intended to create a legacy from property from the start, so getting the structure right to create an inheritance needs planning and consideration. You should have a will drawn up as soon as you have assets to pass on, even if you don't have children. This is a core part of your exit strategy and will help you consider where your money will go when you die.

Aspects to consider when preparing your exit strategy are:

- Why do I want to build a property portfolio in the first place? What are my real reasons for doing this?
- What is my attitude to risk and to leverage? Do I want to pay off my mortgages in my lifetime?
- Will my children want to inherit my property assets? What might be the inheritance tax implications? Will they be prepared to run a limited company in the future?
- When do I need to set up a trust or insurance structure

to protect my assets from the taxman? What would this look like?

- What might the size of my estate be when I die, and how do I want that to be divided up? Are there other people I would like to benefit from my estate?

My exit strategy is simple: death. Blunt, but true. I don't aim to sell any of my properties. I aim to pass them onto my children and allow them to benefit from owning a cash-flowing asset. But whilst I may be rather flippant about my exit strategy, I am aware that this also needs planning so that when I finally pop my clogs, the process of transferring the ownership doesn't add to my offspring's already grief-filled experience of no longer having their wonderful mother around!

It is worth considering your exit strategy when you start to invest in property, especially if you have your sights set on retiring early, passing your wealth onto your children, or creating a vehicle to save tax such as a trust. Property has many possible exit options and it's worth touching on them at the beginning of your journey. If you, like me, have death as your ideal exit strategy, even that needs consideration unless you're prepared for some home truths to be exchanged over your dead body once the family has full knowledge of the complex estate you've created. I would recommend that you speak to a solicitor and tax accountant about your own personal circumstances in light of your plans. It may seem morbid, but as Benjamin Franklin said 'Nothing in this life is certain except death and taxes.'.

ACTION STATION

- Buying an HMO
- Adding Value to an HMO
- Raising Finance for an HMO
- Refinancing an HMO
- Your Exit Strategy

Make a list of the questions that this chapter has raised for you under each of these headings.

What actions do you need to write down now and act on? Make a plan and stick to it. Even if it means getting out of your comfort zone and doing something you would ordinarily shy away from. Speak to five people in the next week about what you're planning to do and open up a conversation about money. Test your pitch and see what results you can achieve. If you don't start now, your procrastination will become a habit. Don't let that happen. Do it before you fear it. That's the way to get results. Plan your exit strategy so you're clear about your direction and focus. This too will help you when you create a JV partnership. Clarity creates momentum. Action creates focus.

CHAPTER 8

FINISH IT

'Give me six hours to chop down a tree and I'll spend the first four sharpening the axe'
—Abraham Lincoln

I love starting new projects. I don't know whether you are a starter or a completer. I am definitely a starter. It's actually really hard for me to keep going once I've started anything that takes more than half an hour. Which is probably why, for most of my life, the result of my production was very little. Songs half written. Book manuscripts nearly done. Goals set but long forgotten. Let's face it, even the four beautiful boys I've brought into the world took about half an hour to create. Yes, there were nine months of brooding and nesting and preparing, but I was fairly passive during that time. It was just the last few hours of those nine months that were the hardest part. Creating them was definitely the best bit!

I have hugely benefited from working with an exceptional team. I have also worked with people who taught me what not to do. After reading this chapter, even if your build experience is limited to Lego, you'll be prepared for managing a build project. Just take it step by step. And let me tell you–if you've ever organised a birthday party for anyone less than eight years old or more than 80 years old, this will be a walk in the park.

To make it easier to plan, undertake, manage and complete an HMO refurb, I use a four-step process:

- Phase 1 – Prebuild, specification and planning
- Phase 2 – Refurbishment, fitting and kitting
- Phase 3 – Decorating and interior and exterior finishing
- Phase 4 – Dressing and photos

If you split the process into sections and define what the triggers are that start and complete those processes, you'll find it much easier to stay in control of the budget, the timescales and the team.

PHASE 1 – PREBUILD, SPECIFICATION AND PLANNING

It's tempting to think that you have no experience that's relevant to project managing a refurb. It's true that many people don't have any construction experience – and you might be one of them. Does that mean that you can't project manage a project just because you don't understand how to put up a six-by-eight timber structured partition wall? No, it does not. What it means is that you'll have to learn the skills and the tools to be able to manage a project effectively without knowing how to build a house from scratch.

This is where your power team comes in. They have the skills and the knowledge to carry out the work, but they will need guidance and management to do this. Project management is not a difficult skill to grasp. However, it requires a rigour and a process that necessitates discipline and application. Without this, your project will easily run out of control and you won't put in place the necessary standards and processes that will help to keep it on track. A project that is out of control will cost you time and ultimately an awful lot of money. In most HMO refurbs that I have managed, overseen or been involved in, the two things that will often overrun are time and costs. The three areas that will affect your project are time, cost and quality. Having a clear perspective on each of these areas will significantly help you control and manage the refurb. If you want to learn more about project management, here are some helpful sites: www.prince2.com and www.apm.org.uk/resources/find-a-resource/agile-project-management.

If you're new to project management and haven't got the time or inclination to learn the theory, how do you avoid running over budget and going overtime yet meeting your quality standards? There are implications for each of these areas if you don't get it right. Income *and* opportunity are lost if your project runs over time and the budget exceeds its maximum tolerable spend. You may be at risk of not getting a licence or refinance if the quality is not right.

If you have no project management experience, I would recommend that you take one of these four options

1. Find a project manager you can work with who has the experience and knowledge to manage the project in partnership with you.
2. Learn project management skills yourself (you don't need to be an expert, but having some understanding of deadlines, workstreams, dependencies and risk

management will increase the chances of a successful project).

3. Work with a builder who is prepared to be the project manager and pay him an additional fee to undertake this role.
4. Use the skills of an architect who is used to working with construction teams to deliver projects on time and to budget.

PROJECT ASSETS

In formal project management speak, there are certain core 'products' (paperwork) that you or your project manager will need to input to at least weekly. These form the key documents that will scope, shape and sustain the project. They need to be regularly updated with feedback from all the key stakeholders, such as architect, project manager, builder and any other relevant contractors. These are:

- floor plans
- the project specification and the exceptions or additions to the specification
- the budget
- the project plan or schedule of works

Floor Plans

There are tools online that you can use to create floorplans such as www.sweethome3d.com or www.roomsketcher.com. If you are undertaking a more complex refurbishment, then it might be worth asking a draughtsman or architectural technician to draw up proposed plans. You will need these anyway if you are applying for planning permission. Otherwise, even in a simple conversion, it's worth having scale plans as you can then plan the refurb and the fixtures and fittings before you get into the detail of the materials and finish. You will need accurate measurements of the house before you start, and an idea of where you want certain items like radiators and doors to be located. You can add in the detail of furniture too, if space is at a premium.

The Project Specification

The project specification is a highly detailed list of all the changes to the property that will be needed to physically alter it into an HMO, excluding soft furnishings and white goods. A good quantity surveyor is essential in your first refurb, as he (or she) will not only be able to create a project specification but also a schedule of works and will advise on the materials and costs, which will give you a guide about whether your builder is on target.

Creating the specification takes time. I usually recommend six or eight hours to get from a blank sheet of paper to a specification you can be happy with. Every room must be considered in detail. Having a video survey of the building available as you write the specification is a massive help. You can hit pause as the camera moves from room to room and you add to the details to your spec. When you are recording the initial video, be sure to pan round the whole of each room and hallway, as well as up and down to incorporate ceilings and floors. Once you have completed the first iteration of the specification, take a good break, preferably at least one sleep, and revisit it. If you can review and explain each portion of the specification to a friend or colleague this helps to sharpen it up. We have found the process of verbal explanation and challenge can hugely clarify the document to the point where it is then useful as a basis for a quote from a builder. You can never include too much detail in this product. You will need to consider:

- Rip-out. What should be removed and what kept? Will you remove chimney breasts and all current plaster back to brick? Or will you try to recycle some of the fittings such as kitchen and bathroom fixtures? What else needs to be removed from the house before work can start?
- Mechanical and electrical infrastructure. Will you install en-suites? Will you do a rewire of the whole property? What broadband infrastructure needs to be in place? Are you fitting TVs into communal areas – in which case have you specified electrical sockets and aerial sockets appropriately in the plan? Will you use PIR (passive infrared sensor) lights to reduce usage in communal areas? How many sockets will be installed in bedrooms?
- Units and sanitaryware. What kind of size and standard of sanitaryware will you use? How many kitchen units and what worktop lengths are needed? How big and what design should the shower cubicles be?
- Design and finish. Do you want extra lighting points in certain places such as over a kitchen island unit? What style of firedoors will you install? Will you be using a variety of paint colours in the final decoration? Where is the flooring and carpet being fitted?
- Even if you're doing a light refurb, consider having all the walls plaster skimmed for a smooth finish, which then creates a perfect finish for your decoration.
- Fit shut-off valves to all pipes that carry water to outlets such as taps, toilets, en-suites and washing machines. Make sure they are accessible if you get a leak. You might want to locate the valves in a hatch or cupboard

that is easy to find when and if disaster strikes.

- Upgrade the loft insulation in the property for a more comfortable ambience – you'll also save on your bills, improve the energy performance certificate of the HMO and have fewer tenant complaints. You may also wish to add further insulation between floors or rooms. If you're adding fire or acoustic plasterboard, this too will add to the insulation in the house.
- When fitting handles and locks to your bedroom doors, use a levered handle which allows the door to remain unlocked unless a key is inserted. Too many tenants lock themselves out of the room in a property if the bedroom has a Eurolock with a snib.
- Windows and doors can be costly to replace but give minimal uplift in value except for improving the EPC of the property. Buying a property with UPVC already in situ will save you time and money.
- Many HMO tenants will use a bike as their main form of transport, so consider where you could install a secure bike rack.
- It's worth thinking now about outside bins and where they can be kept for easy access.

(You can download a sample specification from www.centreround.co.uk.)

Ensure that you speak to your local HMO licensing officer before you complete this piece of work. They will have suggestions and potential additions that you will need to include. Depending on the size of the house and the number of rooms you want to create, you may need to consult the local fire officer too. Housing standards need to be applied to any residential refurb process, although your licensing officer will be aware of Housing Standards and can usually advise you of these requirements alongside the licensing requirements. A document on fire safety requirements is the LACORS guide.[11](Please note that with new licensing legislation this may be updated.)

You will probably need building control sign-off for the work if your refurb is more than simply cosmetic. Ideally, the responsibility for this will be laid at the feet of your builder. However, if you are unsure of Building Control requirements, you can check out the guides at https://www.planningportal.co.uk/ or speak to a local building control team to advise you.

The Budget

Your budget needs as much attention as the specification. If you've never undertaken a refurb before, this can seem daunting, which is why having the support of and advice from a quantity surveyor will be vital. Your QS will be able to advise you on costs for materials and labour and you can use these to plot into your budget. Keeping a weekly check on your budget is a discipline, but one that is necessary to ensure you don't overspend. When you have found a builder that you can work with, and you are happy with their standards of work and the quote, you should have a final pre-project meeting discussing all details of the project including stage payments.

Ideally, payments should only be made in line with work that has been completed. If you pay in advance for any aspect of the build, make sure that this is properly notated and that the builder provides you with receipts, invoices or an email that details what this payment covers. Having four stage payments

11 https://www.rla.org.uk/docs/LACORSFSguideApril62009.PDF.

allows you to keep track of costs and control the expenditure and gives an incentive to the builder to get to the next stage.

If you are using a builder who is VAT registered, ensure you agree on the reduced rate of 5% VAT on an HMO development instead of the usual 20%. However, this depends on the type of conversion you are undertaking and what the use of the property was before it was converted. You will need to have agreement from your builder to charge you at this reduced rate and certain items are not included.[12]

The Schedule of Works (or Project Plan)

This is a timeline that you will create in conjunction with your builder, which will detail the start and end points of the work and the stages at which they will complete. This will give you a structure for your stage payments. A Gantt chart is usually the best tool to use, and you can find tools online. like www.gantter.com, which will provide useful templates into which you can upload your data. You will want to ensure that each stage of the refurb is plotted into the chart to ensure nothing is missed. Here is an example:

1. Demolition and site clearance including garden
2. Joinery and structural work including roof
3. First fix plumbing and electrics
4. Window replacement and external doors
5. Plastering
6. Kitchen and bathroom installation
7. Second fix plumbing and electrics
8. Testing of all services
9. Tiling and final carpentry

12 For further details please see VAT Notice 708: Buildings and construction, HMRC, 2014.

10. Painting and decorating
11. Flooring and carpets
12. Snagging
13. Final completion and handover of all keys, manuals and operations.

[You can download an example Project Plan from www.centreround.co.uk]. Discuss the schedule with the builder to ensure you have accurate and agreed deadlines. That way you can stay in control of the refurb, pay the builder on time, and keep the work accountable.

CHOOSING A BUILDER

With a completed specification, the next step is to seek three or four friendly local builders who can give you a price for the work needed. Builders will appreciate the time you have spent in drawing up a detailed list of the changes that need to be made, as 90% of their clients will invite them to site and just verbally run through a list of the works needed. This leaves far too much room for doubt in any quoted price. Be clear with the builders you meet that the price quoted must be for the list of works needed and that any changes in price will need to be agreed in advance. There are various ways to do this including tendering and interviewing. Ensure that you cover these aspects when deciding who to use:

- Explain about the purpose of the project and ascertain the builder's relevant experience.
- Does the builder have ideas and suggestions about the construction methods?
- If possible, show photos of another similar project.

- Understand if there are subcontractors to be used.
- Ask for insurance details (good reputable builders will have public liability as standard and, if they use sub-contractors, they should also be registered with the Contractor Insurance Scheme
- Ask to see qualifications and proof of membership or registration with applicable trade bodies.
- Ask for at least two people who can give references of other work.
- Give the builder a copy of the plans with any additional notes made during the meeting.
- Agree on a date for a delivery of a quotation.

Getting a quote is the first hurdle to overcome when working with a builder and will demonstrate how committed and keen they are to work with you. If they don't hit their own deadline for the quote, this can be an indication of their general attitude to time-keeping. There are other aspects to consider when choosing a builder such as:

- Price
- Previous track record on similar projects
- Quality of work
- Attitude
- Communication skills

Price is only one of the factors we review when selecting a builder. Be wary of quotes that seem way lower than competing quotes. It doesn't mean that they are invalid, but it is useful to understand the reason the quote is so much lower. If the reason is that some fundamental aspect has been left out, it is better to know that at the start of the process than in the middle. Builders tend to walk off site when they discover this kind of problem. Once you have selected the builder you will use for your HMO refurb, there are other factors to consider before you allow them to start work on site:

- Contract with your builder that they will be responsible for health and safety on site. Under CDM Regulations (which are national guidelines for ensuring health and safety on a building project site) there must be someone on site who has health and safety at the foremost of their minds. The builder should be contracted to take on the role of CDM lead designer and CDM lead contractor. Works must be notified to the Health and Safety Executive. Examples of responsibilities include ensuring there is a working toilet, drink-making facilities and running water. Signage may need to be displayed, depending on the level of work being carried out, and tasks such as tidying up cables and debris, and having a first aid kit, also need to be covered. Your builder should be well-versed in CDM as this is the national standard for construction projects.
- Agree a start date with the builder and also an end date. Agree a reporting structure with the builder so that each week he or she is duty bound to send a short written report detailing highs and lows of the work completed. In conjunction with your project manager, you need to crystallise what has been done each week and what has slipped or is lagging behind the project schedule.
- Check their insurance is valid and appropriate. They should carry public liability as a minimum.
- Ensure you have the correct property insurance while work is ongoing and the building is empty.
- Get a coded keylock installed somewhere discreet on an outside wall of the property. The keylock is a small

lockable steel casing that can only be opened by way of a code and can be attached safely to a front wall or brick facing. A front door key is safely placed inside and the code is only given to those you approve. So instead of having lots of keys cut and managing them, you just tell the latest workman or contractor what the code is and they can let themselves into the property. Don't remove it when the project is over, as you can then continue to allow maintenance contractors to use it when necessary. The code will need to be changed occasionally to ensure the ongoing security of the property.

PHASE 2 – REFURBISHMENT, FITTING AND KITTING

As the project lead, and the one ultimately responsible for the project budget, your overall role is to control the project by monitoring, managing and feeding back issues to the builder you see. This is achieved by careful reference to the build specification and timescales agreed. You, or the project manager (and who is not the builder themselves) will need to attend site regularly (at least weekly) to ascertain what progress is being made.

Here are things you should keenly address:

- Work not starting on site, on time. This is an early indication of lack of builder prep and organisation. If there is a serious hold up at the start, consider telling the builder that the contract is lost and he should consider the relationship at an end. Builders who start seriously late rarely get back on track.
- Quality levels slipping. You will need to be on site regularly to ensure that you see the many aspects of the

work by the builder. Ensure corners are not being cut to enable on-time completion.

- Lack of progress/lack of staff on site. For a decent-sized refurb with an 8- to 10-week build phase, there should be staff on site nearly every day of the working week, often more than one staff. If this is not happening, it should ring alarm bells and you will need to speak rapidly with the builder to find out what the problem is and ascertain if slippage is occurring. If the slippage gets serious, end the relationship with the builder, pay what you fairly believe you owe and restart the work with another builder.
- You should never pay for work in advance. If the builder asks for this then walk away. On the other hand, it is quite reasonable and normal to agree that you will be paying for the work in stages, as the stages get completed. As an example, you may wish to agree that once stages one and two are complete, a payment can be made. Before you make the payment, ensure the works are complete to the stage agreed and to the agreed quality standard.
- On site you should have a hardback A4 book, which is used to note any changes/additions to the build. Whenever a change in the specification is identified, someone notes it in the book. When you (or the project manager) are next on site you need to agree the changes and the cost increase, and sign this off.

I would also recommend that you decide from the start which tools you will use to manage the project and how you will communicate as a team. Examples are Freedcamp, Slack and WhatsApp.

- Freedcamp is a basic online task manager. It is great for handing out tasks to each project team member and tacking completion.
- Slack is a relatively new tool in the market and has a number of features, which include inter-team chat, document handling and task tracking.
- WhatsApp is completely free to use an provides rapid communication either person to person or within predefined groups. WhatsApp does not provide document-management capabilities.

There are hundreds of great tools available on the internet for project and team communication. But there is danger in trying to use all of them in one go. Pick one or two that look good and stick with them. We have seen many a project go awry because of the use of too many different, incompatible tools! As you generate project documentation, be sure you have backup copies to fall back on and test these out from time to time. There is nothing worse than losing a huge raft of important project details midway through a project. It can cause a huge loss of confidence in all concerned.

If the works you are carrying out require inspection from the local building inspectorate (give them a call and ask them if you are unsure) then you need to be clear with the builder that this is fundamental to your payment/s for the final stages of the project. We always place a high value on testing of services in the HMO, a long time before the builder leaves the site. This testing should include running all taps simultaneously, testing of all plug sockets and kitchen appliances that have been installed. Any other mechanical or electrical items should be tested so that any glitches can be dealt with within the original build timeline.

I often get asked about how we design our HMOs to ensure that hot water and cold water are in plentiful supply for our tenants, even in the larger HMOs. The answer is that it is complicated! In the largest HMOs I would advise using a bespoke mechanical and electrical engineer to ensure that the design is right. In HMOs with up to six or perhaps seven en-suite bedrooms, you can often get away with using a pressurised hot water tank and perhaps a few electrical showers. But this does create risks without a proper plan. You have been warned! But this topic is worthy of a conversation with your builder to ensure he/she understand what you need and that you will be testing the functionality at the end. You may wish to write into the refurb spec that the risk of the final system not working is with the builder – set out how many showers you wish to run for how long simultaneously so that everyone is clear what criteria must be met.

At the outset of the project, it is very much worth agreeing a payment structure with your builder that envisages retention of around 3–5% of the build cost, well beyond the end of the project. This allows for you finding issues with the build (and there are always some) and then being able to get the builder back on site to fix the issues. We usually agree to release the final amount owing for the refurb at nine months after completion of initial snagging.

Most projects have five stages that align with the structure of the refurb and give clear stage payment dates (you can align this on your project plan as well):

1. First fix
2. Second fix

3. Plastering
4. Decoration
5. Snagging

It's worth holding back about 5% of your budget for snagging. This will ensure a builder is incentivised to complete the build to the required standard. You should have a thorough snagging procedure at the end of the refurb, which will allow you to assess whether the project is ready for handover or not. The budget should also include a 10–15% contingency in the case of emergencies and unexpected extras.

PHASE 3 – DECORATING AND INTERIOR AND EXTERIOR FINISHING

Interior design in HMOs has markedly shifted in the last few years. Since investors grew more aware of the demand for high quality accommodation, for which there was a paying audience, they've realised how potent a feature wall can be to their bottom line. Good interior design is a mixture of an art and a science and, despite what some may think, consists of more than the choice of which should be your feature wall. There are reams of books and online articles about effective interior design, many of which are neatly illustrated with reference to real interiors – just the kind of pictures you will be perusing to decide exactly how to create your own special blend of HMO. Eclectic, modernist, neat, minimal, urban: all variations on a theme – how to create an attractive and unique property that will rent well for many years to come. If interiors are not your thing, do not be perturbed. This section should help you crystallise exactly what works and what is unnecessary fluff.

Consideration needs to be given to the overall image or 'feel' of your property, the needs of your tenants, and pure practicalities that make the HMO work as a home. Each room, whether it is a bedroom, living room, kitchen, shower room or even outside area, should be considered as part of the overall property design, and should add to a sense of flow between the different areas of the house. The parts to consider are colour, furniture, amenities and accessories.

INTERIOR DESIGN

In an HMO it is a good idea to create a scheme that unifies the whole house, yet also separates individual areas by colour. Do this by using a similar neutral colour throughout and highlight feature walls with paint colour or wallpaper. To unify the whole house, keep all the woodwork the same colour. If you are going for neutrals on the walls, get some paint mixed up for the woodwork that is a ratio of one part of the neutral colour with three parts white. You can use the same shade on the ceiling. Don't forget the colour on the opening side of the door into the next room – it doesn't have to match but pick a shade that won't jar.

Decide which of the two colours you want to feature more. If you use them both in equal amounts, they will fight for attention and cancel each other out. If you're nervous about using dramatic colours in reality, try introducing a complementary scheme in the form of a throw or accessory before you go ahead with an actual paint colour. You can use a third colour – preferably in a different tone from the other two, but don't have more than three colours. Balance the scheme by introducing some neutral colours as well such as cream or white. Pairing one dark and one light tone of each of the two colours can work well. Experiment with it in both combinations, for example try a light soft grey with a vibrant deep pink. Then try it the other way around – put together a deep slate charcoal grey with a sugared almond pink. If you have followed the advice above around choosing a suitable backdrop as a colour scheme, you'll already have the canvas upon which to build the layers that make for your unique look.

Here are my top 15 tips for designing a long-lasting yet impactful HMO interior.

1. Use a maximum of three colours for the base colour palette and three colours for highlight or feature areas. The base colours are used for the walls and woodwork and the feature or highlight colours can be used to pick out certain walls, or areas of space that can be particularly striking. Colours can take quite a bit of time to choose as there are a number of considerations in creating the perfect colour scheme. After designing the colour schemes for a number of our HMOs individually I realised that having a repeatable and consistent colour palette meant that I wasn't spending hours in my local paint centre analysing reams of paint colour strips.
2. Consider using the services of an interior designer for your first HMO as they are trained to draw out the features of your decorative design through the careful arrangement of objects such as mirrors, pieces of art, soft furnishings and removable dressing items. They can create a business 'mood board', which you can then use time and time again.
3. Repeating elements such as colour, shape or texture

can help to unify a space and create a consistent visual experience. Paint, tiles, carpet, flooring and wallpaper are all really easy ways to create repetition.

4. Pay extra to have built-in furniture. Using the skills of a good quality joiner, you will generate a bespoke feel that utilises space in the most efficient way. Built-in furniture reduces damage, increases storage and lasts much longer even than reputable landlord furniture packs.
5. If you do use a landlord furniture pack, try to create some variety in the way you dress the rooms. Being able to give rooms separate identities (through colour, arrangement or accessories) makes them feel more individual and less institutional.
6. Use anti-mould paint in the kitchen and bathroom or anywhere that might be exposed to dampness.
7. Use quality carpets and luxury vinyl tile that create a seamless, contemporary and very hard-wearing surface. Floors make up a large proportion of the living area of your property and you'll end up replacing the nasty stuff in a few years anyway when it's tired and scruffy.
8. An alternative neutral scheme using slightly darker colours is more functional than magnolia and white. These show scuff marks more readily and are also very overused. Soft sheen emulsion is cheaper than durable acrylic matt and is just as durable and washable. Always take a note of all the colours and RAL (specific paint numbers) you have used so that you can buy small tester pots for touch ups when necessary.
9. Larger wall tiles in kitchens and bathrooms look dramatic and attractive and are faster to cut and fit. Take some samples from a tile show room to test in your property

before you decide. Shower panels are an alternative to tiles, They are easy to clean and require no grouting and therefore won't attract mould.

10. Beds need to be a sound quality divan or base and always use a good quality mattress with a mattress cover (fitted just before a tenant moves in).
11. When planning the layout of furniture in a room, it helps to have templates you can move around to assess the space. If you've used an architect to draw up plans, they may have added furniture icons to the plans. If not, create your own templates using weed suppressant material that you can deftly move around to ensure the right placement of furniture.(Go to my YouTube channel to see a video explaining exactly how to do this.)
12. Upgrade the loft insulation in the property for a more comfortable ambience – you'll also save on your bills, improve the energy performance certificate of the HMO and have fewer tenant complaints. You may also wish to add further insulation between floors or rooms. If you're adding fire or acoustic plasterboard, this too will add to the insulation in the house.
13. When fitting handles and locks to your bedroom doors, use a levered handle that allows the door to remain unlocked unless a key is inserted. Too many tenants lock themselves out of the room in a property if the bedroom has a Eurolock with a snib.
14. Fake leather sofas may seem a good idea at the time, but after a couple of years the fabric wears, the faux leather creases and it ends up looking tired and worn. Rather, buy a fabric sofa that is covered in hotel-grade upholstery and that you have treated with fabric protector. This is much easier to upholster should the need

arise and is ironically easier to keep clean.

15. Download a comprehensive shopping list from www.centreround.co.uk to equip all your bedrooms and communal areas, such as bathrooms, kitchen and lounges. Having the essentials for tenants when they move in makes it much easier for them to settle in and stay. However, you can be assured that, within a few months, their items will blend with yours. So do a full inventory as you shop.

Now it's the turn of the removable elements that can really draw the eye into your spaces and have tenants racing to book a viewing.

PHASE 4 – DRESSING AND PHOTOS

Once the property is completed and every room now has walls, floors, ceilings finished and completely decorated, all fixtures are in place and all mechanical and electrical items are in situ and tested, you're ready for the fun part (well this is the part I find the most fun!). Choosing furniture and buying all the extras for your HMO takes time, but it is where you get to choose the final look and feel of the property. If you have planned this well from the start, you'll know exactly what 'look' you're trying to achieve – whether its edgy and industrial, homely and soft, or chic and cultured. Some of the aspects of style should already be in place – the colour scheme, the pieces of furniture, the individual look. If you have created a mood board this will now start to be more focal in your work as you buy and source items that fulfil this image. There are a number of excellent HMO furniture suppliers who can help you create beautiful rooms and sell furniture packs.

If you decide to dress your rooms yourself, and you're not familiar with interior design concepts, I'd suggest that to keep up with trends in interior design, there are a number of websites and online sources that you can consult. Pinterest, Dulux, B&Q, and Homes and Gardens are just a few of the websites that will show contemporary interiors and fashions. Dressing a room is all about creating the 'wow' factor, whatever the base background colours might be. There are certain interior design rules that will help you dress rooms and ensure that you aren't limited to simply throwing a couple of cushions on the bed. These are rules which are easy to implement and will enable you to maximise the features and benefits of the rooms you're dressing.

As human beings, we are drawn to symmetry. To do this in your HMO find the focal point of your space, which could be the bed, a large window or even a large piece of art. Not something functional like a door that has no aesthetic appeal. In a kitchen this might be the cooker, or a breakfast bar. Then evenly arrange objects on either side. Make sure these are either identical or of equal visual 'weight' (weight depends on size, colour and texture, e.g. black has more weight than grey). You could also try asymmetrical balance – rather than mirroring items, play around with a slightly off-balance combination of weights, colours and textures. You might choose to use items such as large mirrors, cheap canvas paintings, tall and short plants, artifacts and decorative items that you can find cheaply in stores such as Asda, Dunelm Mill and The Range. Dressing a room is about creating a visual impact that draws the eye and creates an image of a lifestyle. Too organised and controlled will make a room feel clinical and too much personalisation will make it feel cluttered. Getting that balance right takes time. You may need to have a few attempts at dressing a bed or organising a kitchen to get that feel just right. The principle of harmony provides the 'full stop' to any interior design – when harmony is in effect, the space should feel complete because all its parts relate to, and complement, each other. This feeling is the result of balance, scale, proportion and repetition all being used in the right amounts. Harmony is the measure by which we judge whether a space works or not. One of the very easy ways to draw a space together harmoniously is in the use of soft furnishings like cushions, throws and rugs. Because they are removable, you can arrange them and reuse them. These items can also provide the perfect splash of colour to an otherwise bland canvas. Even in rooms that are slightly dated in appearance can benefit from an orange splash of colour provided by some bright, oversized cushions, a large rug, a bowl of oranges placed discreetly on a dresser and a large orange picture hung above the bed. After you've taken the photos you can of course remove these items if you wish. We leave pictures as they brighten up a room, but usually remove soft furnishings, as tenants have their own bed linen.

Try experimenting with different proportions of items within a room. Pictures above a headboard or bedside lights are good examples of where you can go wrong with scale. Too small and the pictures will look lost on the wall. Too big and they will dwarf the room and become too dominant. Try a series of pictures above a bed that are slightly smaller than the area covered by half the equivalent area of the headboard. Arrange them by width or height and remember the symmetry rule to ensure a pleasing composition. Ensure bedside lights are in proportion with the headboard.

Once the interior is dressed, clean and ready, pay attention to the exterior of the property. Sweep, tidy, arrange and dress – in exactly the same way as you have inside. Make sure your kerb appeal is as swanky as your kitchen. Once you are happy with the dressing and layout of the rooms, now it's time to capture the property inside and out with great photos.

PHOTOGRAPHY

Now the house is completely ready and fully dressed, set aside some time (or pay a professional) to take a full series of photographs, detailing all aspects of the HMO. Effective property photography involves a little planning, time and applying the right techniques to get the best results. Photos should sell your listing and help to create a story. They need to show the property in the best light and appeal enough to get tenants to visit in person. Here are ten tips to ensure that your photos show your property off as aesthetically as possible.

1. Use a DSLR camera. The biggest error many agents and landlords make is using poor quality images. Especially with low-cost listings, many agents think it is acceptable to use grainy images, which often results in room voids. Property advertising requires high quality images. Smartphones and basic point and shoot cameras just don't provide this. To get the images required for effective marketing, you need to use a DSLR camera. Research shows that listings shot with a DSLR camera gain more interest faster than those that were not. Learning how to take your own photos isn't hard; it requires the correct equipment, some practice and knowing basic techniques to get started.

2. Attach your camera to a tripod. Hand-held cameras are great for taking spur of the moment pictures, but a tripod will give you the stability to take clearer, sharper photographs.
3. Switch on all the house lights. Even during the day, having all the lights on in the property will instantly make it look warmer and more appealing. Switch on all bedside lights, draw back and straighten curtains and blinds, and turn on any en-suite lighting. Lighting makes a huge difference to the appeal of an image. If there isn't enough light then the photo will appear dark and grainy; too much light and the image will be over-exposed, reducing the amount of detail visible.
4. Avoid reflections. There is nothing more unprofessional then flicking through images of a listing and seeing a reflection of someone in a bathroom. All good photographers have the skills to avoid getting their reflection, and that of a flash and the camera, in a shot. Try using different angles in a room that has reflective surfaces, like kitchens and bathrooms, to reduce the chances of getting caught in the photo. Sometimes it isn't possible to completely avoid a reflection, especially in small, tight spaces. All you need to do is take your photo as normal, then use an image editing service to remove the unwanted reflection. Sometimes it's impossible to avoid catching your reflection in an image. Another suggestion is to set up the shot using the self-timer on your camera, then step out of the room.
5. Use lighting equipment. Dark corners don't do an HMO any favours online and simple lighting equipment will help you illuminate them. A flash will help, as will a reflector and even a light stand.

6. Use a bubble spirit level. To prevent your pictures looking wonky, use a bubble spirit level to ensure your camera is perfectly angled for each room.
7. Take exterior shots in the morning. Getting up a dawn isn't everyone's idea of fun, but it's the ideal time of day to get the best photographs of the outside of a property: dawn light is better and there are fewer people around. Watch how the light hits the property. At different times of the day, and at different times of year, the light will change how the house looks.
8. Process the images. Processing helps to soften, sharpen and generally tidy up any imperfections. Using online tools, you can sharpen, blur, soften and lighten shots, adding to the quality. Be selective in the images you use, and only include those that show the good features of the property. All the images used should tell a story and add value to the property – you want to show off as many features as possible in the most appealing way
9. Take a photography course. If you plan to take your own photos and know your skills are not up to scratch, there are photography courses run at adult education centres all over the country. They are the best place to start learning about taking better pictures.
10. Use the services of a professional photographer. Good quality photos can make the difference between your rooms renting quickly or not. With a one-time investment in professional photographs, you can reuse them each time you come to let the property. Even if your agent offers to take photos, I would still recommend you take a series of your own. Then you can decide which ones are of a higher quality for advertising purposes.

ACTION STATION

- Phase 1 – Prebuild, Specification and Planning
- Phase 2 – Refurbishment, Fitting and Kitting
- Phase 3 – Decorating and Interior and Exterior Finishing
- Phase 4 – Dressing and Photos

What aspects of 'Finish It' do you need to tackle first? Where can you apply your current knowledge and skills to build projects even if you've never undertaken a construction project before? Make a list of tradesmen that you'll need and create your own database of contacts. Start to draw up all your project assets and work on them one by one until you have a complete set of project management tools.

Don't let this part of your HMO strategy go awry. Remind yourself of the vision and, with that, you'll find the energy, focus and operational ability to undertake the most incredible refurbs. You are creating a highly worthwhile product that will last for many years. Get it right and you're creating a golden goose – get it wrong and you could lose many thousands of pounds. Prepare, plan and execute.

CHAPTER 9

FILL IT

'Debt is good only as long as there are tenants to pay my mortgages. If tenants stop paying their rent, my good debt turns into bad debt'
—Robert Kiyosaki

The way to fill rooms in the contemporary HMO market is not the same as letting a house in the traditional lettings market. Dominant websites such as Rightmove are still useful portals, but they should not be the sole funnel/pipeline for finding your tenants. To fill your rooms fast and cheaply is an ideal that many HMO landlords wish for. The reduction of voids and maximisation of occupancy should be at the top of your agenda at all times. Only with customers buying your product do you have a business, and now that you have created a wonderful home for tenants to live in and enjoy, it would be a complete waste not to have those rooms rented out. Renting out rooms successfully requires a systematic process, but also a good eye for what works, and an awareness of tenants' preferences. That way you can ensure your marketing messages will hit the spot. If you do decide to use a letting agent (and please make sure you follow the ticklist below to suss out the wheat from the chaff) you might even want to share these ideas with them. You may have a great interior, with all the latest amenities and gizmos but you now need to ensure the property meets its sole purpose – to create rental income. For this you need to fill your rooms with paying tenants.

There are three aspects to renting your rooms fast:

1. Preparation to rent
2. Marketing, advertising and sales
3. Seven-step system

There is quite a debate about whether you should personally manage your HMO properties or whether you should hand them over to an agent. Part of the due diligence you did earlier in the book was to ascertain what level of involvement you want in your HMO once it is up and ready. Some HMO experts will tell you that you can only make it work if you commit to managing the properties yourself. Personally, I think that is an old-fashioned view that comes from people who haven't learnt to leverage systems, tools and their team. It is an area worth considering early on. When I started investing in HMOs and developing a portfolio, I quickly realised that I had absolutely no desire to rent my rooms myself. Initially there was no choice and I had to lead this process. There was simply no-one else to do it.

I then resisted setting up the lettings side of the business, as I am not naturally a good process person. I thought it would take me too much time and trouble. What I knew was that I needed help; the person who came to my rescue was in the form of a young woman who was looking for some extra part-time hours. She has been with our company now for four years and I can honestly say that she was my saviour. Being a person who is good at dotting 'i's and crossing 't's meant that she finished off all the jobs that I had left undone. Her general positive demeanour and sense of humour often kept us both sane! She followed a process and improved it, and she helped me keep our rooms full. It seems to me that if you do decide to run the whole gamut of HMO tenanting, you need a Jennifer too.

If you can't find a member of staff as good as our Jennifer, then the only way left to you is to use an agent. The reason we started doing this ourselves was purely because there were no HMO agents around at the time. We tried the services of one local letting agent for eight weeks when we were on holiday. With just three rooms available I could not understand why a few weeks later all the rooms were still empty. When I returned from my holiday, I filled them in four days.

USING AN AGENT

If you decide to use an agent, you need to know that they have the knowledge and experience to let and manage your rooms effectively. They should understand national legislation and local housing policy (some of which is outlined below). They have to be registered with the Property Ombudsman or the Property Redress Scheme and have registered for the Client Money Protection Scheme to hold rental money on your behalf. They should be registered with the Data Commissioner's office to hold electronic data and have a privacy notice on their website. As well as knowing about legislation and how to rent to a tenant, you need to assess how well an agent can evict a tenant if there are problems; how responsive they are to tenant's issues; and what systems they have in place to deal with emergencies. As with all business partnerships (and you should consider your relationship with your agent as such), knowing and liking each other helps make the relationship run smoothly. Rather than sound as if you are interviewing them, and basing your decisions purely on price, it's worth taking some time to understand what their values are, such as transparency, speed of reaction, and communication levels. For example, we always set up a WhatsApp group for any new property we take on as an agency. This means that all day-to-day issues are dealt with in conjunction with the landlord.

Here are a list of questions to prompt your thinking about what you need from a local agent:

1. What experience do you have in renting out HMOs? What is the type of HMO you specialise in?
2. What is the average room rent you achieve?
3. What is your average void period?
4. What is your average type of tenant?
5. How do you advertise the properties?
6. On average how long does it take you to rent a room?
7. What percentage of rent advertised do you achieve?
8. How many licensed HMOs do you manage?
9. Are there any additional charges for managing a licensed HMOs?
10. Do you have a list of charges for your services?
11. How do you deal with maintenance and repair jobs?
12. How do tenants contact you for emergencies?
13. How do tenants report issues or general queries?
14. How often do you or your team visit the property?
15. How do you deal with rent arrears or missed rent payments?

16. How do you ensure the cleaner is managed well?
17. Which KPIs (key performance indicators) do you gather and supply to your clients each month?
18. What is your inventory process?
19. What advice would you give to an HMO landlord?

LEGISLATION

Keeping abreast of changes in the legal requirements for renting property can be time-consuming. However, understanding key pieces of legislation is essential to protect yourself, your business and your tenants. A good lettings agent will inform you of changes, and give you a general overview of the law. It is still your property and, therefore, your responsibility to ensure that you are legally compliant. Knowing the basics of the relationship between the landlord and the tenant will ensure that you stay on the right side of the law. There are plenty of books and online material you can access to learn more about this in depth. By following the seven-step system to systemising listed below, you'll ensure that your legal duties are executed.

This is just some of the legislation that govern the practice of the PRS:

- Deregulation Act 2015
- Electrical Equipment (Safety) Regulations 1994
- Energy Performance of Buildings (Certificates and Inspections) Regulations 2007
- Furniture and Furnishings (Fire) (Safety) (Amendment) Regulations 2010
- Heat Network (Metering and Billing) Regulations 2014
- Houses in Multiple Occupation (Management) (England)

Regulations 2009
- Housing Acts 1996 & 1998
- Housing Act 2004
- Landlord and Tenant Act 1987
- Licensing and Management of Houses in Multiple Occupation and Other Houses (Miscellaneous Provisions)(Amendment)(England) Regulations 2012
- Licensing of Houses in Multiple Occupation (Prescribed Descriptions) (England) Order 2006
- Anti-Money Laundering Act 2018
- Redress Schemes for Lettings Agency Work and Property Management Work (Requirement to belong to a scheme etc.) (England) Order 2014
- Regulatory Reform (Assured Periodic Tenancies) (Rent Increases) Order 2003
- Rent Act 1977
- Smoke and Carbon Monoxide Alarm (England) Regulations 2015
- Tenant Fees Act 2019
- Town and Country Planning (Use Classes) (Amendment) (England) Order 2010
- Town and Country Planning Act 1990.

This list is not exhaustive (although it is exhausting!). At the time of writing, the government has announced a review of the Housing Act 1998 and a proposal to remove section 21 – the process to evict a tenant from a property in what is considered a 'no-fault' eviction. This itself demonstrates the flood of changes being made to the PRS. If you are new to the legal requirements of renting, I would suggest you sign up to an online service such as Tessa Shepperson's landlord law blog: https://landlordlawservices.co.uk/. Your local council may run an accreditation scheme for landlords, which is worth joining to receive the regular training sessions that are often run and that focus on legal compliance.

PREPARATION TO RENT

When I was a little girl, my mum would sometimes say to me 'Wendy, your dress looks pretty, your shoes are polished and your cardigan is neat. But remember 'a woman's hair is her crowning glory'. At the age of five I had absolutely no idea what she was talking about so my look of puzzlement would mean my mum had to issue a more direct command: 'Go and brush your hair'.

Now that you have created a fantastic house share, with all the amenities that tenants could want or need, it's time to 'brush its hair' and create some crowning glory. If you have decorated with a well-chosen colour scheme and used the principles of interior design in the previous chapter, then preparing the house to rent will be easier. If you have an agent, or a member of staff who will be letting the rooms, it's worth running through this process with them. Let them understand what your systems are, so that together you can create a repeatable process.

To finalise the property for the new inhabitants that you will entice easily into their beautiful new surroundings, now is a good time to carry out the following preparations:

- Ensure that all the systems have been tested to the 'n'th degree, for example:
    1. put all showers and taps on and run the washing machine simultaneously.

2. turn the heating on to maximum
3. turn on a number of electrical appliances to check for short fuses.

- Compile a complete set of spare keys for each room, and all external doors and windows. All keys should be labelled (even if you are using a masterkey system) and any copies placed in a lockable cabinet in a separate office.
- Gather together all the appliance information leaflets and warranty information in a separate folder.
- Create a tenant's information folder with local information such as local transport maps, doctors' surgeries and supermarket locations.
- You can array the house with too many signs. So make it neat, accessible and legal by creating framed noticeboards with the following signs:
  1. House rules
  2. Emergency contact details
  3. Wifi log in details (and user policy if you have one)
  4. Bin collection times (you can download these from your local council's website)
  5. Fire exit information
  6. The HMO licence (if it needs one)
  7. Gas and fire safety certificate.
- In addition to a fire escape notice on the general noticeboard, all bedrooms need to have a fire escape notice locally. Depending on the complexity of the fire escape route, you may also want to put up fire escape stickers that clearly show the escape route.
- Any starter cleaning materials provided to be in place under the sink.
- Bins clearly labelled for recycling or general waste

(interior and exterior).

- Bike racks installed.
- Clear house number signage at the front of the property.
- All areas cleaned, tidied and smelling fresh (including outside).

MARKETING, ADVERTISING AND SALES

Collins Online Dictionary defines marketing as 'the action or business of promoting and selling products or services, including market research and advertising'.[13]As in all businesses, the ability to get your product or service to your market is vital if you are going to be a profitable venture, which is where effective sales and marketing kicks in. In the early days of HMOs there were limited ways in which a landlord or agent could market their properties. Few specialist HMO letting agencies existed, so often landlords would market and rent their rooms personally. Strategies included advertising in local papers, placing cards in local shops and post offices, speaking to local employers and, of course, in the student market being on the accommodation officer's preferred list.

Sites such as Spareroom, Openrent, and Roombuddies now offer the landlord a way of describing the unique features of their property and uploading photos as visual evidence of the room and property on offer. So how do you ensure that your rooms have the impact in your advertising that will encourage your potential tenants to take action?

13 *Collins English Dictionary,* complete and unabridged 2012 digital edition.

There is without doubt a science to formulating copy for advertising that works. That formula is constantly being tweaked by the fashions and language of the marketplace, which is a reason to stay in touch with the culture of tenants to whom you are renting. For example, over the last few years in which I have been growing and developing my HMO portfolio, I have noticed that tenants are just as happy with smaller bedrooms if there are additional benefits to living in the property, such as superfast broadband, great additional storage solutions, plenty of sockets in their room and places to charge tech gear. When I started out, it seemed that unless a room was at least 15m^2, tenants were put off by the lack of space. However, now, there are additional services and benefits that we can offer that may make up for a smaller bedroom (while meeting minimum room sizes of course ...).

En-suites, good lighting and double beds are now much more in favour over communal lounges that are not communal, dingy lighting and large but dreary and uninviting kitchens. Knowing this about your potential tenants means that in your marketing, you can address these preferences and ensure that these are the benefits you highlight. Just like a good artist, your insight and recognition of your market will lead to innovative ways to reach that audience.

The first step in telling people that your rooms are available is marketing. If your marketing is not up to scratch, it doesn't matter how good your rooms are. You simply will not be able to get the right tenants at the right time paying the right amount of rent.

In a less competitive market (as was the case a few years ago) it was possible to fill a room from an advert in the paper and get five applicants for the room. Is this day and age, filling rooms is more challenging. So, as well as ensuring that your rooms target the right market, you (or your team or agent) also needs to be a master of marketing, to tell the world what you have and how they can benefit from it.

AIDA

The rule of thumb used by marketing experts across the world when formulating copy for adverts is found in a simple acronym – AIDA.

- Attention
- Interest
- Desire
- Action

Attention

How can you grab someone's attention? A piercing headline, an interesting image, a shocking statement, an attractive photo ... You really only have two media that you can use – words and pictures. But effective use of these media can stimulate sight, sound, touch, movement and even taste. Grabbing the attention of your market in a competitive industry requires knowledge, insight and awareness. What do your current tenants (or those you hope to rent to) do for a living? What are their hobbies and out-of-hours activities? How do they spend their free and leisure time? What excites and stimulates them? What motivates them to spend money? Knowing this level of detail about how your potential tenants live, work and play can transform your marketing strategy immediately to make it more effective.

Capturing someone's attention starts with two things – appealing images (video and photography) and engaging headlines. Once you have a series of excellent photos, showing off the interior and exterior facets of the property, you will need to choose a series of these to showcase on your website, any other website portals and social media sites. The range should include:

- Individual bedrooms and a feature photo shot to showcase the standard of all the rooms
- Bathroom/en-suite
- Kitchen
- Social area (lounge, kitchen/diner)
- Outside area/front of house
- Additional bedroom shots

By identifying a core selection of photos for each property, and having a handful of shots per bedroom, you will have a useful compendium from which to choose each time you create an advert. These photos can also be used to create video compilations and graphics that you can use on other advertising literature.

When it comes to writing an advertising headline to sit alongside your photos, these too need to demonstrate your affiliation with your customers and grab their attention:

'Unhappy and fed-up with where you live? Let us transform the way you feel', 'Beautiful and spacious room ideal for your needs. Plenty of sockets and great wifi', 'Sick of your current landlord not fixing problems? See the difference renting from us makes', 'Beautiful rooms at Fantastic Prices'.

Interest

Once you have someone's attention through your headline, photo or product promise, your next step is to pique their interest with more details. Here you will describe in more detail the room, the house, the area or location and what facilities your HMO provides. In advertising copy, you have the space to really explain in depth why your house is ideal. Remember to focus on the benefits and not just the features. For example:

The location – what are the benefits of living in this area?

The layout – why this gives space, storage and independent living.

The careful choice of other tenants – how this ensures happy and peaceful co-living.

If you can explain the benefits to a tenant, rather than just the features, they will understand more readily why your HMO is preferable to another HMO.

Desire

Marketing works by creating feelings in your potential buyers. Usually, these are feelings of desire or want. Regularly you'll see adverts in which feelings of need and incompleteness are emphasised. You're made to feel that without that item/service/product your life is unfulfilled. Sometimes adverts stimulate the emotions of shock, surprise or pleasure. Successful marketing works when you take action because of how you feel about what you read or saw. Much of the success in marketing works by telling a story– a story of someone you can relate to, who is much like you in many ways, yet didn't feel quite complete without such-and-such a thing. Hey presto, that thing appears, and the person feels much more complete, whole, perfect and happy. Bingo! I'm sure you've experienced many of these pieces of marketing, and can recall the more memorable ones that made you laugh or cry.

What stories are you telling in your marketing? What emotions are you creating in your potential tenants? If your copy is all fact-based you're missing a real trick in being able to tap into the emotions of your potential tenants.

Tip: Spareroom has created a useful wizard for tenants looking for somewhere to live in London. You choose a number of descriptors that matter to you and then appropriate adverts will be shown to you. Wherever your HMO is located across the country, this is a fantastic tool if you are struggling to describe your property fully. You can include these descriptors in your advert and boost the interest in your HMO: https://www.spareroom.co.uk/flatshare/where_to_live_wizard.pl.

Action

A call to action is often one of the least used advertising techniques, and yet one of the most effective. Your audience needs to know what to do once they've decided they're ready to explore and examine your HMO rooms more thoroughly. Ensure that you include a simple call to action at the end of your advert:

'Call now to book a viewing xxxxxxxxxx', 'Email or text immediately to secure a time for your viewing xxxxxx', 'Don't miss out on renting one of these rooms. Book your slot now xxxxx'.

Urgency and scarcity are oft-used tactics to get people to take action. So you may want to point out how fast your rooms rent and how few are left in this property.

ONLINE MARKETING

One of the sites that is used most extensively for letting rooms and finding rooms to rent is www.spareroom.co.uk. Search Google for 'rooms to rent' and it's very likely Spareroom will come to the top of your search string. Founded by Rupert Hunt in 2004, Spareroom has undoubtedly been a driving force in allowing investors to have an insight into current market conditions for rooms in the UK. Initially this led to a swathe of investors recognising the unique and valuable information that no other site was offering and allowed them to see untapped areas where there was demand from tenants. Investors flooded into larger conurbations, and quickly benefited from the knowledge that Spareroom gave them. The transparency of the site also allowed tenants to compare and contrast local property and gave them access to a much wider choice.

Spareroom has evolved over time to adapt and change to the marketplace. Having secured its position as number one for advertising in a fairly niche marketplace, there are only a few other sites that offer similar services (roombuddies.co.uk being one). However, the advertising pricing structure of Spareroom can be costly and it lacks transparency as to how customers (potential tenants) view the listings, so it's challenging to assess whether the advert you have paid to be at number one is really at number one when a new tenant hits the site.

You will need to create an account with Spareroom and then you'll be offered a choice of advertising packages. There are various options including early bird and bold advertising levels. Prices increase with the level of adverts and number of properties you place on the site. Spareroom changes its features from time to time and making sure your advert is at the top of the listings is crucial to its success. I'd recommend that you scroll through the information pages on Spareroom to understand its bells and whistles (and you can check out my YouTube channel where I regularly post about Spareroom – https://www.youtube.com/user/wendywl).

There are other portals that you can use to advertise rooms, such as Zoopla, Rightmove, Gumtree and Openrent (which posts to the first three when you use their paid option). Openrent has additional features, such as reference and credit checks, which you can pay extra to access. The benefit of Openrent is its tool for posting to other platforms that would otherwise require an extra monthly fee. It's also worth exploring other local service websites and portals specifically for your area as these can be useful additional places to advertise. Keeping on top of new portals that show up on a Google search can prove very effective: often these are new sites that have paid to be at the top of Google listings and are prepared to allow you to advertise your rooms more cheaply, because the site is new and needs advertisers.

The use of social media as a tool for finding and advertising rooms has become far more prevalent over the last two years. In Best Nest™, we have found this to be as effective as advertising on Spareroom and Openrent, and it's likely this will eventually overtake portal and website advertising. Many HMO investors and agents are using a combination of social media sites such as Facebook, Twitter and Instagram to advertise their properties, where they can showcase their latest property trends and developments. They have found that these are more organic and can reach people far faster for less cost than other forms of traditional advertising.

If you are renting your own rooms and haven't yet got business social media accounts established, this should be your priority. Setting up a Facebook page for your business will allow you to create adverts specifically targeting your demographic and, if you wish to increase the reach, you can pay for Facebook to run a campaign for your rooms. The ability to pinpoint people in your chosen location within certain parameters (age, gender, income) is a game-changer when it comes to targeting your ideal tenants and allows you to track the impact of your advertising spend.

You also need a company website. Despite the trend in social media advertising, your website acts as a shop window and should not be a tool to be ignored! Your own website doesn't have to be expensive or complex to be effective. Having a simple WordPress site allows you to showcase your rooms, your brand and your properties, in a way that is more static, yet accessible. Ensure it is fully mobile and GDPR compliant, so that you can capture the details of interested tenants and respond to them quickly.

OFFLINE MARKETING

As well as having an online strategy, offline marketing should also be a consideration. Leaflets, postcards, posters, and even banners will add more presence and awareness of your rooms locally. These can be placed in shop windows, gyms, takeaways, and other places that tenants frequent. Signage outside your HMO can be used (your agent may ask for your permission to put up signage). Check what the local council rules are, as you can fall foul of local planning policy unwittingly by having signs up perpetually.

Using both online and offline marketing combined, you'll be able to raise awareness of your rooms and also create a buzz about your brand. You may wish to run campaigns occasionally, if room sales have slowed. These can be in the form of discounts, vouchers or special offers. Developing partnerships with other local businesses helps to raise your profile and also enables you to benefit from referrals and mutual support. Recruitment specialists and agencies, warehouse operations and large employers are often the best businesses to approach to tell them what you do and to offer your rooms to their employees. It can take time for them to see you are serious and committed in what you're doing. Don't give up if you find you don't succeed first time round. Our best business partnerships have taken time to develop: both parties need to see a demonstration of longevity to create trust. Each partner needs to see that the other will deliver – you to provide great rooms at reasonable prices, and them to provide suitable referrals.

Don't forget that tenants can also be a valuable source of referrals. Create an ongoing referral scheme that pays out for any new room rental: it's a powerful way of thanking tenants and also allows you to measure how they think of you!

SEVEN-STEP SYSTEM TO RENTING ROOMS

There are seven steps to finding tenants, which ensure a non-stop supply. This system also ensures your rooms are ready to let out again once a tenant leaves. The steps are:

1. Reach
2. Respond
3. Reference
4. Rubber-stamp
5. Rent
6. Refund
7. Review

REACH

This is covered in the marketing and sales section in more detail. In essence, this step covers how to *reach* your tenants. Using the methods outlined above, this step allows tenants to find you and contact you and you to reach out with your product offering (your rooms).

RESPOND

Unless you have a speedy way of responding to a tenant's enquiry, you are likely to lose their interest. Ensure that you have phone cover 24 hours a day using a telephone answering service or virtual office system. Email, text and messages need to be responded to as quickly as possible to ensure you find tenants who are right for your property. Before you arrange a viewing, it's worth asking them a few pre-qualifying questions such as:

- When are you looking to move?
- Where are you living now?
- What do you do (as a job/occupation)?
- Where are you moving from?
- Have you lived in a shared house before?
- Do you have a budget and, if so, what is it?

Save yourself viewings time by pre-qualifying the tenant on the phone before you book a date for a viewing. On the day of the viewing, always text or call the tenant an hour beforehand to confirm the viewing. Turn up to the house at least 15 minutes beforehand to ensure it is ready.

This next tip is taken directly from my previous book, *101 Essential Tips for Running a Professional HMO*:

'During the viewing, make sure you are friendly and open – ask questions of the tenant as well as showing them round. You may need to undertake some sales training if you are not used to selling, as not only do you need to "sell" the house and the rooms to the prospective tenant, you need to be able to listen to their needs and match the offering to what they want. It is really important at this stage to create a conversation rather than an inquisition and as you listen to their answers, you can use these to "help" the PT [Prospective Tenant] choose your room over others they might see. You will want to find out:

If I ask for a reference from a past landlord will I get a good report? (A very telling question.)

Do you have any CCJs [county court judgements] or outstanding debts that I need to know about? (A key question that enables you to identify their honesty as you will discover the truth when you reference them.)

Do you smoke? (Not necessarily a deal-breaker, but nevertheless useful to know.)

What are you ideally looking for in a property? (A great opportunity to match the features of your property with their preferences.)

Have you got a girlfriend/boyfriend/partner? (Useful to know in case of long-term sharing risks.)

My rooms rent really quickly and I already have another couple of people who are really keen to view soon, so why should I choose you over them? (A direct question which will give you a real insight into the real person!)

Finally use your gut instinct. If you don't think this person is right for the room or the property, it's always better to be honest. If you need some time to think about it, make an excuse like "I have another couple of viewings later and I really promised to show the other people round, so I'll call you later to discuss the room if that's ok?" Then call them and be frank and let them know you don't think they are right for the house and the reason why.'

If the tenant decides to take the room, you should take some form of payment to secure the room and remove it from any further advertising. From 1 June 2019 you cannot take any fees for setting up a tenancy, even for referencing and credit checks. You can ask for a proportion of the deposit up front to secure the room, which is then deducted from the overall deposit when the tenant moves in. Collect information from the tenant (you will want to create an initial application form) that outlines their basic information and referees. The information you should gather needs to include personal details such as name, current address, telephone number and email; their job and salary details and National Insurance number; the details of referees and in what capacity are they known by the referee; and information about identification being provided. Then they need to sign the form and agree to continuing with the process for becoming a tenant (i.e. having a credit check undertaken).

REFERENCE

References give you assurance about your tenant and ensure that they will be able to pay the rent and be suitable for the property. If you have doubts about a tenant, you do not have to accept them as a tenant in the property. However, assuming they have passed the initial stages and you are happy for them to rent a room it is vital to carry out references. There are five steps you can take to check out a prospective tenant. The first three are essential and the other two are optional depending on your time and resources. There are a number of online services that will carry out references for a small charge, such as www.lettingref.co.uk, www.landlordreferencing.co.uk and www.vanmildert.net.

Credit Reference

If you're not happy about the results on your tenant, you may decide to insist they have a guarantor. This is a vital aspect of the referencing process as it allows you to see if the tenant has any CCJs or other formal financial claims against them which they should have already disclosed.

ID Checks

You should verify that your prospective tenant is who they say they are. You need to see identification (ID) with a photo such as a passport or European-style driving licence along with another form of ID such as a utility bill.

Bank Statements

Ideally your tenant's income should be two and a half times the rent – so if the rent is £100 per week, your tenant should be earning £250 per week. To demonstrate this you will need to see the last three months' bank statements, which also provide an invaluable insight into the financial position of your prospective tenant. Is the tenant paid what they say they are? What are the tenants' regular outgoings? Do they regularly get overdrawn? If the prospective tenant refuses to show their bank statements, they may have something to hide, in which case you have a right to be wary.

Employer's Reference

This should simply confirm the employment status of the tenant – is the tenant employed where they say they are? Importantly, is the prospective tenant on a full-time contract or is their temporary contract just about to finish? It should also give you their salary details which is useful in assessing the tenant's ability to pay.

Personal/Business References

When an applicant is currently living in rented accommodation it is useful to obtain a reference from their existing landlord. I would suggest asking the landlord:

- How long has the applicant for the tenancy been a tenant of the current landlord?
- What is/was the rent paid to the current landlord?
- Was the rent paid in full and on time each month to the current landlord?
- Were there any periods where the rent was in arrears?
- Is the rent currently in arrears with the current landlord?
- Has the applicant for the tenancy cared properly for the investment property and its contents?
- Would the current landlord accept the applicant for the tenancy as a tenant again?
- It is always better to call and speak in person to a previous landlord as it is quite possible for tenants to create a previous landlord's reference.

You may want to discuss your findings with the prospective tenant and ask for more detailed information. You may also wish to ask for the details of a guarantor to guarantee their rent should anything go awry.

Once the referencing has been completed communicate with the tenant about their next steps and make arrangements for them to move in.

You will need to be registered with https://ico.org.uk/ to store data electronically. This site will also help you with a privacy policy for your website in line with GDPR regulations.

RUBBER-STAMP

Before moving in a tenant, you need to 'Rubber-Stamp' the tenancy legally by issuing a number of pieces of information to the tenant. These are:

- Assured shorthold tenancy suitable for an HMO (in which the inclusions and exclusions are defined)
- How to rent guide
- Inventory of their room including contents and condition (take photos for evidence)
- Gas safety certificate
- Electrical safety certificate
- EPC
- HMO licence.

These can all be electronically issued. You may want to use an online signatory service like www.signnow.com to make it faster. The assured shorthold tenancy should be signed and returned before you issue keys and carry out an induction into the property.

In addition, I would suggest you create:

- A welcome pack, including emergency contact details
- Useful information
- Local guide

When you move a tenant in, you will need to carry out a short induction that explains the operational parts of the house such as:

- House rules
- Wifi details
- Gas and electric meters

- Stopcock in the event of a flood or leak
- Bins and collection times
- Storage queries
- Cleaning up
- Bikes and parking rules
- Any other local regulations or issues they need to be aware of

Communicating with tenants regularly takes time and effort but can rapidly reduce the amount of hassle and time that is spent managing the property *and* increase the length of their tenancy. Simple steps like a monthly group email (try mailchimp.com) lets your tenants know that you care about the quality of their experience in the property. We have found this reduces rather than raises queries, as tenants then understand procedures and policies more clearly and also what kind of behaviour is expected of them!

RENT

Take the first month's or week's rent before you move a tenant into your HMO. Set up the tenant on your online system and create a corresponding invoice on your online accounting system. This way you can reconcile your rents easily each month. It helps if you can get all the tenants to pay on the first of the month, to make reconciliation faster. Staying on top of rental payments is a core monthly task. You can of course outsource this to a bookkeeper or virtual assistant. You should make it a priority to check rents and assess the profit and loss of your business monthly.

REFUND

When a tenant leaves your HMO, ideally you will have at least a month's notice (stipulate this in your contract). Ensure you have as robust a check-out process as your check-in process, so that the leaving goes smoothly and the room is then ready for the next tenant. On the agreed date that the tenant is moving out, you need to meet the tenant at the property and check the room and inventory. Ensure you check *all* areas such as the kitchen and utility/laundry areas and any outside shared areas. If all has gone well, the rent is up to date and the room is left clean and tidy, then you can return the deposit to the tenant. However, if there are arrears on the account you will need to ask them to pay the arrears before they can receive their deposit back. The best way to avoid this is of course to manage arrears as soon as they arise. Don't let tenants fall behind with their rent without addressing the problem and, if that means taking legal action, then you will need to do just that.

REVIEW

Once you know a room is about to become available, prepare to advertise it as soon as it becomes vacant, ensuring the photos and information are up to date. It is always a good idea to refresh the room and carry out any upgrades at this point. Use your contacts database to advertise the room and email those people who initially showed interest a few months previously. You never know whether their situation has changed and they now need to move. Your room might be just what they need now!

By following each of these seven steps, you will have tenants all year round and need never experience voids or issues. In the next chapter, I'll discuss how you can now Future-Proof your HMO to ensure it runs smoothly and continues to be a high cashflowing asset.

ACTION STATION

- Preparation to Rent
- Marketing Advertising and Sales
- Seven-Step System

Decide which route you will take – self-managing or using an agent. How will you choose your agent? Are you prepared to get into the detail of what they'll offer to support and help you?

Which parts of the Seven-Step System to renting rooms do you need to study in more depth? How will you prepare your information and keep it readily available? How will you store data?

Make a list of registrations you need to activate for further advice and compliance information.

https://landlords.org.uk

https://www.rla.org.uk

https://ico.org.uk/

Setting up these aspects of your business are just as important as finding the property and finding the money. Set aside some time to do it so that you're covered and ready to go.

CHAPTER 10

FUTURE-PROOF IT

'If I had asked people what they wanted,
they would have said faster horses'
—Henry Ford

In his famous book *The E-Myth*, Michael Gerber emphasised the importance of systems as a core business focus if your business is to scale and grow and be protected from the winds of change. When I first came across his book (along *The E-Myth Revisited*) I was struck by how differently I had approached my own business growth. I was definitely in the category of the hapless entrepreneur – great ideas and vision, lots of energy and potential, and happy to talk to investors all day long. When it came to systems and processes though, this was my weakness and I knew I needed help.

After months of buying, developing, refurbishing and managing my HMOs I began to realise that I had created another part-time job – one that had no set hours, no set patterns and no sick pay. The benefit was that it was also unpredictably passive too. So, I would have days when there would be little happening that needed my attention: I ran the portfolio with little fuss. Occasionally a tenant would give notice; I would organise the move-out and start to advertise for a new tenant. Then at other times I would be faced with a torrent of questions and issues – from wifi not working properly, to questions about rent payments, and issues with cleaning and tenant behaviour. I had wondered about using a local managing agent but, quite frankly, there were none locally that were as good as me at filling rooms, and none that had any kind of online systems that I wanted to emulate.

The fluctuations in my working patterns made it impossible to plan when I would be busy and when I would be free, thus impacting every area of my life. My family was relatively patient. But at times the weekends could be taken up problem-solving a knotty HMO issue – much to their annoyance – leaving mum tired and stressed.

By 2015 I was managing over 60 rooms plus our single-let portfolio. Far from being passive, I was very active. I had been able to finally let go of my part-time hours at the university, leaving me more time to concentrate fully on the HMO portfolio. We were continuing to grow the business through further purchases. So, I was often needed for viewings, site visits, meetings with builders and project update calls. I was regularly on the phone to my business partner, Mark, ensuring that we had covered all bases to create a sustainable and profitable business. His role was finances: mine was operations. I felt like I could audition as a juggler in a circus, with every plate that I was spinning simultaneously. Time was pressured and I was also trying to be a good mum to my boys, keeping them well and safe, helping them with homework and occasionally making time to actually play and talk with them! Andy was working away from home Monday to Friday, and my life never seemed to stop. If you are at this stage in your business, you'll know exactly how it feels, and how your time is constantly pressured. This is where Future-Proofing comes in. The aim is to take you as much out of the day-to-day operations of the business, allowing other people to do the roles that you don't want to do, so that you can concentrate on what you're good at.

If you grow your business anything like as fast as we did, you'll find you have income but little time. The growth of the business meant that within just three and a half years, we had created enough income for Andy to resign from his well-paid contracting role. It was a job he had come to loathe. Working away from home in a highly pressurised environment had sapped his spirit. It was a tremendous moment when I was able to call him and let him know that, on the latest figures from our accountant, he could immediately resign. We had achieved our goal: £5,000 residual income per month. This monthly income figure would allow us to focus solely on the business without having to hold down other jobs. It was only a start, but it was our financial freedom figure.

You might think that it is at this point when my story ends. Indeed, when you reach your financial freedom figure you might think that's where your story ends. But you'd be wrong. For it is in the next part of the system that the magic really lies: It is in the ability to systemise and remotely manage your portfolio where the lifestyle is created. Too many investors miss this final step and end up where I was: busily managing their portfolio and wondering how it differs from having a well-paid part-time job. They are making extraordinary profits from ordinary property but the day-to day job of running the portfolio means that they are on-call constantly, without people or processes to free up their time.

MY SECOND EPIPHANY

It was a Monday morning in May 2015. Having left his contracting role, Andy was ready for a new challenge and, boy oh boy, did I have something which with to challenge him! What I didn't realise was how much this would test me too – but how much this would change our lives: the process of Future-Proofing.

Sitting in our home office at his tidy and well-organised desk, Andy glanced over at *my* workstation. Covered in post-it notes, mortgage application forms, tenant applications, and ASTs waiting to be filed, his withering look told me all I needed to know: this was *not* what he had envisaged working with me would be like.

'Babe', he said sympathetically, but with a mildly patronising tone, 'do you think this is how we should run this business?'

'Uh, what do you mean?' I asked.

'Well, I just think that unless we make some big changes around here, we'll both end up with another job. I mean it looks like that's what you've done already. How can you even see your way ahead when you organise your paperwork like that?'

I looked down at my desk and across at his. I had always played the creative card, pleading that tidiness was not compatible with being a visionary. He wasn't just referring to the multicoloured arrangement of post-it notes attached to my computer screen. This was about organisation and leveraging our time. This was a resource that I was wasting and, with fresh eyes, Andy could see how it was being wasted. There was no point in creating a fantastic recurring income stream if we couldn't systemise the business. We would end up swapping our time for money and losing the freedom that we believed in so dearly.

I felt pretty bad as he pointed out that my disorganisation, and paper-strewn workstation, was probably costing us money and time. I knew I was not the tidiest person in the world, but I had never thought that my ways of working were that bad. Andy's background in banking and IT had given him an advanced knowledge of systems, which was what I needed now. I was all over the place and it was no wonder I felt lost. Inside I felt angry that he could confront me about my productivity, as without my efforts we wouldn't be sitting here at all. I also realised that, despite creating a residual income stream, there was no point if we couldn't enjoy it by reclaiming our time.

'Thanks very much' I shouted, sarcastically. 'If it weren't for me, you'd still be working for a living'.

Andy could see I was upset. 'Yes, that's true. But now you and I need to go up a gear. We need to create a systemised business that works without us. If you want to travel and do all those things on our bucket list, it's not gonna happen doing things the way we are now.'

'Alright, smart ass, what do you suggest we do differently?' I objected bluntly.

'We have to plot out our business. Piece by piece we have to lay out what we do and how we do it. We notate it all into a flowchart. Then we write up the flowchart as a business manual. This will become our operations manual. Then we can hire people to run the business for us. We'll have a paper-free operation. We'll use simple online tools and reduce our time each month working in the business. You might even get round to writing that book you keep talking about.'

I encountered the reaction that we all feel when we know something new is about to occur – that magnetic force of resistance. The power that holds us back from changing our lives and our habits. Internally I felt a dragging and undeniable resistance. I was not only offended at my husband's audacity to criticise me – I was hurt that he saw something to improve. I felt vulnerable. That was the truth, and it made me feel like a failure. I took it personally that the business was not being run as well as it could. As my ego descended its haughty mountain and calmed down, I began to contemplate the suggestion of a root-and-branch systems review.

The light began to dawn. I envisaged a desk with no paper, and a diary with space to do other things, like speaking and writing. Maybe I could even start to help other people create HMO businesses. I could make an impact in a bigger way. It was completely out of my comfort zone, but I trusted Andy to steer our course. His ideas were right – we needed to grow a team and create processes to make this work without us! I knew that if I listened and learnt, this could really help us achieve the freedom that I ached for.

'Wow', I thought 'this could change everything'. I wasn't going to admit to him that I was thinking that though.

'Well', I said, 'it's your turn to start the ball rolling on this one. You can be responsible for getting all our processes and systems to work. I've done the core part. Now it's your turn.'

The gauntlet was thrown down and, with alacrity, Andy swept it up.

'There are three areas we need to concentrate on – getting paying tenants, ensuring the properties are looked after, and running the business profitably. If we can do all three, we're onto a winner'!

SYSTEMS THINKING

I learned that a business built on systems has added value. Indeed, no business that has ever gone public did not have repeatable, predictable systems thinking at its core. Take McDonald's as an example. Their core business is all about systems and property. Did you think it was about food? Ray Kroc, who took the fledgling yet already automated McDonald's business to new audiences across the globe, and made his billions doing it, saw that it was the combination of a product that people enjoyed and would buy repeatedly, with an experience that was unique, and a system that was repeatable. The McDonald brothers had systemised their original hamburger restaurant to a 'T' and, if popular history is to be believed, Ray Kroc was so astonished by the potential that the McDonald's brothers didn't have the vision to see, he immediately set to work duplicating the same model of restaurant over and over again. Ray

Kroc was undoubtedly a man of great ambition, and it was his recognition of the value of the systems that the McDonald's brothers had created (which he himself might have struggled to create as he was primarily a visionary and a branding expert) that gave him the idea to build on the strong foundations and expand the business rapidly. Over time, through the franchise network that he built, he recognised that McDonald's was not a hamburger chain but was a real estate business. The global growth of McDonald's wouldn't have happened if their systems were not developed, tested, refined and exploited for growth.

In your business there will be core areas that require systems to let them run smoothly and efficiently and also allow you to scale, by being controllable and ordered. What are the core reasons for having systems in your property business? Systems can save you time (as long as they are efficient), they can create a brand (as long as they are consistent) and they can reduce friction (as long as they are predictable). So, I want to explore here these three qualities of business systems that have a direct impact on outcome.

In your HMO business you will be bombarded with hundreds of pieces of information per day – whether it is new HMO deals, investors who want to work with you, tenants who have questions, data about new areas in which to invest, or news about the wider economy. Each of these pieces of information creates bits of data that need to be sorted, codified and stored somewhere. Sounds very technical but that's exactly what our brains do whenever it comes across a new piece of information. These bits and bytes of data travel across our brain's neural networks at the speed of light, allowing us to learn the consequences of thoughts, reactions and decisions. We use past experiences to furnish our memory, to change and affect how we react in future. Our brains are masters at sorting information, storing it and recalling it.

When it comes to the paperwork in your business, categorising it and slotting it into a logical system is not always as straight-forward. For a moment, consider what kind of information you might process in your HMO business. Here are some examples:

- Property details
- Transaction paperwork
- Financial statements
- Funding calculations
- Mortgage offers
- Estate agents' information
- Vendor information
- Bank details
- Utility information
- Insurance quotes
- Builder's quotes (and those of any trades you work with)
- Projects information
- Bills and invoices
- Staff costs
- Tax returns
- Company documentation
- Legal and regulatory processes
- Contracts
- Maintenance processes
- Terms of engagement
- Tenancy documentation
- Personal identification documentation
- Financial measurement tools

... and many more.

When you first start receiving these pieces of information, it can be hard to immediately categorise, codify and store them. They end up as a heap of paper on your desk, or a load of unread emails in your inbox (which was the state mine was in back in 2015). A further problem is that this kind of approach means that only *you* can deal with the information, as there is no logical system that someone else can learn. One of the main drivers to systemise our business was that we wanted time freedom as well as financial freedom. In order to fit everything into the same time that you have every week, your focus on systemisation is the key to growing your operational capacity.

I am *not* a natural systemiser. I am not an engineer and, if anything, find reverse-engineering a bit of a mental block. I can create, and inspire, and sell – but systemise? You've gotta be joking!

Two years in and I realised that, with all the running around I was doing, I had to address this area of the business. So, with the support of my mentor (who also did a great job of marriage guidance) (!), I chunked up each step of our HMO process from scratch and devised my simple Five-Step System. This became the backbone of our Organisational Operations Manual and we use this daily to run the business. It has taken us from disorganised chaos, which ate up our time, to streamlined processes where staff carry out the majority of the day-to-day operations. Now, I spend far less of my time in the business and can stand back and lead and manage the team. This is not only more satisfying from a time and routine perspective, but it also allows me to use my skills better in negotiating, building partnerships and networking (where I am definitely stronger naturally anyway).

Another aspect of building a systemised business is the ability to create a culture where time is valued and relationships are nurtured. It allows you to be a better leader when you have predictability in your business and where core systems are under some kind of control. Don't make the excuse 'Oh, we are in start-up phase so everything will be in a mess'.

1. Efficiency

The questions that help ascertain the efficiency of a process are:

- How much time does this process take?
- Who needs to be involved in this process?
- How many staff need to be involved to carry out this process?
- How many other resources are needed?
- What tools can we use to get this done faster?

Property is a people business and, even with automation and the amazing tools that can improve efficiency, there is a level of interaction and team work that is core to making property work. One area that I think has masses of room for improvement is conveyancing. This process is one that you will be involved in regularly if you are buying property and for which you will use the services of a conveyancer or solicitor. One of the core commitments we resolved to have in our business from the early days was to be as paper-free as possible One of our key mottos is 'scan, save, shred', which allows us to keep all documentation in an electronic format and never lose a single item of paperwork. We use a desktop double-sided scanner which then saves all paper documents and allows them to be filed in our Google docs folder structure. Then the paper is shredded. However, there are professional experts whom you will have a need to interact with who haven't yet realised the benefits (or application) of having a paper-free operation.

If you can take one aspect of your business, such as conveyancing, and analyse it using the questions above, I suspect there are other ways you can create efficiencies. Repeat this with other aspects such as finance, advertising, tenanting, sourcing and soon you'll find you can start to leverage your time. There are many online tools that can help you in each area of your business, such as CRMs (client relationship management) i.e. Infusionsoft, Active Campaign and Zoho; online file and folder systems (Google Drive, One Drive, Drop Box); online accounting software packages i.e. Quickfile, Xero, or QuickBooks; and online tenant software programs. Another motto we have held dearly to is using 'lo-cost or no-cost' solutions.

Whatever tools you use, ensure they fit with the flow and needs of your business. Just start with one process and systemise it after flowcharting the process.

2. Consistency

To create a reliable brand that consumers recognise and want to use and be associated with, you need to ensure there is consistency in your product. I speak of HMO rooms as a product and customers as consumers, because that is exactly where the advancements in HMO delivery are heading.

> *'We see our customers as invited guests to a party, and we are the hosts, so it's our job every day to make every important aspect of the customer experience a little bit better'*
> —Jeff Bezos, CEO and Founder of Amazon

To develop consistency, you will have to repeat your processes a few times first to understand where the weaknesses are in the system. Consistency does not need to mean bland monotony either. It is the consistency of the approach and the ability to implement a decision or choice consistently that is the focus. So, for example, in HMO number 1 and 2 you might decide on a fashionable grey colour scheme, decorating woodwork in a particularly luscious shade of charcoal. The walls might be dove grey and the ceilings painted in cloud white. Does consistency mean that all your properties henceforth need to adopt the same colour scheme? Absolutely not. The consistency in your procedures is around the process you adopt to choose the colours, communicate them to the painter and decorator and assess them afterwards. Storage of all the data created is vital. Use a tool that is backed up regularly and accessible by those who need to access, update and export the information.

3. Predictability

If you are great at starting up, but not so good at finishing, this will seem akin to monotony. I would like to reframe that in your brain. Predictability doesn't mean that you have to eliminate variety, choice or creativity. As someone who loves variety and finds it hard to stick to systems, I've had to go through a mental shift to embrace the value of predictability. When you understand and know what is happening in your business, it brings stability and a foundation for growth. In a start-up business the first few weeks and months are always unstable due to this being a period of initiation. It will pass as you define and redefine your core business. So be patient if you love systems – you will be able to create systems that control your business in time. If you are a creative type who loves to disrupt and work in a more haphazard way, this is the time to revel in the energy of birthing something new.

Once you know and understand your core business purpose – such as producing high quality rooms for high quality tenants – you can start to clarify what systems are going to be core to your ability to run the business effectively.

THREE CORE AREAS

Our motto is 'hands-free and happy', which means that any process, system, tool or function needs to be systemised to the degree that we can run the business from anywhere in the world, no matter what time zone we're in. It's been liberating! We've travelled extensively across Europe in Max, our motorhome, and had weeks out of the UK at a time in further flung destinations, knowing that the business is being looked after by our team, and following the systems that we've put in place. On mapping out the areas of the business that needed consistent attention to ensure turnover and profit (Future-Proofing), we noticed that they fell into three areas:

1. Maintaining customers
2. Managing the property
3. Maximising profits

If you can create systems and processes that attend to all three aspects, you will have a portfolio that gives you income and time. This is the central engine that delivers your lifestyle goals.

MAINTAINING CUSTOMERS

By investing in an HMO that will be rented to a professional or working tenant, it's worth remembering that you are renting to a sector of the marketplace that may be working in a sales-driven, customer-focused environment. If you don't provide great customer service and value for money, your customers will look elsewhere. I use the term 'customer' deliberately, because your tenants *are* your customers. They buy from you for at least six months (if not nine months or more), and each month they pay you for the room and house. It is therefore your responsibility as the landlord or investor to ensure that they get the very best service they can.

If you are using an agent to rent your rooms, this is an excellent way to leverage your time. Ultimately, though, the property is your responsibility. It can be very easy to stand on the sidelines and criticise an agent for lack of performance, but there could be a valid reason why your rooms haven't rented as fast as you would like. Running an agency now I can see both sides of the argument. Good communication, regular feedback and fast attention to issues will enable you to develop a productive working relationship with your agent.

By future-proofing our HMOs and keeping tenants happy, our average length of let is 18 months and our occupancy rates are 92% (calculated by how many days per annum a room is vacant). Retaining customers takes time and effort, but you'll find that as you do this you will remain optimally attractive to new tenants too. When rooms become vacant it will be easier to advertise them well and fill them too because you will have remained on top of your business and not let it get on top of you!

Ensure you stick to the Seven-Step System for renting your rooms as described in the Fill It chapter. In addition, ensure you communicate regularly with your current tenants. Inform them when you or your team will be undertaking routine checks and give them at least 24 hours' notice when you need to enter their room (this is determined by the tenancy agreement).Treat your tenants well and you'll have a much greater chance of avoiding problems.

It's likely that at some point you may have to evict a tenant or chase a bad debt. A spreadsheet is your best friend when it comes to ensuring you are compliant with legal processes. There are proprietary software systems that you can subscribe to, but we use Google sheets, forms and docs for everything. We use a pre-tenancy tracker for collecting information before the tenant moves in, and a tenancy tracker for their details once they've moved in. Using a Google form you can automatically populate this information quickly and easily. Keeping well organised with data is half the battle and, that way, you can stay in touch with tenants in a two-way flow of information.

MANAGING THE PROPERTY

It is imperative that you create systems for managing all the health and safety aspects of your HMO (especially if it licensed). These need to cover fire alarm testing, emergency lighting testing and health and safety checks. As a manager of an HMO you are required to:

- provide essential contact information to each occupier
- take safety measures (such as fire precautions, escape routes etc.)
- maintain water supply and drainage
- supply and maintain gas and electricity
- maintain common parts, fixtures, fittings and appliances

including any garden, which should be kept in a safe and tidy condition
- ensure that each unit of living accommodation within the HMO and any furniture supplied with it are in clean condition at the beginning of a person's occupation of it and that every window and other means of ventilation are kept in good repair
- provide waste disposal facilities

Regular checks on the general standard of the property will help you nip problems in the bud and keep it looking tip top. We have a master maintenance tracker that allows any reported maintenance issues to be RAG rated (red- high importance, high urgency; amber – medium importance, high urgency; green – low importance, not urgent). Maintaining a list of local tradesmen is vital to ensure that you always have people to call on to undertake maintenance tasks. WhatsApp is a useful tool for communication and coordination.

We use a masterkey system to keep the number of keys to a minimum and, alongside this, we have a regular key audit to ensure we have copies of all keys for all properties. All houses have copies of keys in coded keylocks to reduce time for call outs when tenants lose their key (which happens fairly regularly).

Try to find a tenant who will take responsibility for 'low-level' aspects of house management such as waste organisation, bulb replacement and communicating of other problems that need addressing. We call this person the 'lead tenant' and they receive a small payment of £15 per month as a thankyou. We have a role description outlining the duties of this person to clarify what is expected. I have found this works really well in ensuring that there are sufficient bin bags, washing up liquid and other cleaning consumables, that the bins get put on the street and collected once empty.

A call-answering service is another huge bonus when running a hands-free business, as it allows your team to be able to take calls in their time. Any emergencies are now handled by our out-of-hours service and fed back through the maintenance systems the next day.

Having the detail to hand about the interior fixtures, locations and unique idiosyncrasies of your HMO is essential if there's a leak, or a lock breakage or a wall gets scuffed. You can quickly locate the data relating to that property and ensure that the handyman attending to the job has the correct information. Our master maintenance tracker has an additional tab, which keeps track of *every* code, log in, paint colour, key location, meter location, stop cock position of each property. Using a Google sheet is infinitely more flexible too as it allows you to add a column for a new type of data should you find you need it.

Property management should be reactive and proactive and having both types of systems running will allow you to maintain great houses and high rents.

MAXIMISING PROFITS

A motto we have held to closely is 'lo-cost or no-cost' solutions to maximise profit. Maximising your profits to ensure a steady stream of repeatable residual income is the goal. You can do this with ordinary properties as you've already seen. If you're spending the extra profit on fancy tools and systems though, you will rapidly reduce the 'head height' that allows you to reinvest, grow the business or draw income out. As I have already referred to, we base all our processes on Google. They have some wonderful tools which are completely free to use, and integrate with many other add-ons such as Zapier, which can connect to a number of apps in a row. You can create simple automations in Google docs, sheets and forms to manage the day-to-day admin of the business. In addition, the two extra tools you will need and which Google doesn't yet handle are online double-entry bookkeeping services (such as Xero, QuickBooks or Quickfile) and a CRM.

If you want to travel the world, write books, spend time with your family, get fit, run another business or just explore your dreams, then you'll need to bring other people on to help you. There are many ways to do this without having to employ people, and you can be as smart about this as you are in the other areas of your business. While the business needs managing, it doesn't have to be you who does this. Creating a 'future-proofed' property portfolio with ordinary properties for extraordinary profits also means being clever and creative in how you run it.

Suggestions for maximising your profit include:

- Create key performance indicators that you regularly assess, such as cashflow, profit and loss, overall balance sheet figures, occupancy rates, time on the market before filling, cost of advertising, your time input, monthly maintenance costs and yield. Some of these KPIs can be analysed annually, others quarterly and some monthly. Keep an eye on your business statistics so that it is controlled, measured and tweaked where necessary.

- If you are using the skills and time of other people, either as contractors, service providers (such as a VA or PA) or employees, ensure they report to you their key results areas on a weekly basis. With this information you can then identify where time and money is being lost and where their skills are most useful and effective. And remember Sheryl Sandberg's famous words when it comes to choosing a member of your team – 'Hire slowly, fire quickly'.
- Each time you readvertise a room, consider adding a few pounds per week increase to the price. A small amount will not affect your enquiries, but it will increase your bottom line.
- Collect rents on time and regularly check them with your online accounting system. Each time you create a new tenant entry, you can create a recurring invoice (which doesn't need to be sent to the tenant). This then allows you to reconcile with actual income in your business bank account. Even a few days of late payments per month will make all the difference to your cash flow.
- Create a late payment policy. Although you cannot charge fees to set up a tenancy, you can charge for chasing rent and late payments. Decide at what point you will go down the route of evicting a tenant, and keep abreast of the legal process by becoming a member of the Residential Landlords Association or National Landlord's Association. They have helpful guides and legally compliant forms and letters you can use. Having a policy means you can remove the emotion from the process and outsource this to a member of your team.
- Assess your regular outgoings such as utility bills, insurance, broadband and mortgage costs. Reducing

bills, even by 5–10% per annum will compound your cash flow and profits. Does your cleaner need to come weekly or could fortnightly be enough? Are all the bulbs in the house LED?

- Take regular meter readings to assess usage. If bills are rising fast you need to investigate and identify why. There are a number of devices available that allow you to control the heating and temperature (often the largest jump in bills is due to additional heating. Tumble dryers are a common culprit for rising electricity bills). Are there appliances that could be linked up to a coin-operated meter and cover the cost of use?
- Keep an eye on new technological developments in the HMO industry. Whether it is a new piece of software that can help notify you of late rent payments or an app that can control your heating remotely – use technology to systemise your business, thus saving you time and money.

ACTION STATION

- Systems Thinking
- Maintaining Customers
- Managing the Property
- Maximising Profits

Which of these areas are you already ahead on? Do you have your online folders and structure set up to organise your HMO business? What action steps do you need to take now to improve this? Which days of the month will you oversee your property performance?

Who do you need to help you now?

Is there additional hardware or software you need to help with the business? Are there any specialists you should be connecting with to outsource and run the operations of your business? What tools would help you regain your time and free up your headspace?

FUTURE TRENDS

CHAPTER 11

SCALING UP

'If your business depends on you, you don't own a business – you have a job. And it's the worst job in the world because you're working for a lunatic'

—Michael E. Gerber

Developing an HMO business that works so that you don't have to is the ultimate golden goose. By feeding it the right nutrition at the right time, the goose lays golden eggs each month – the unequivocally ideal residual income generator. The question is, what is the nutrition your HMO golden goose needs? Just like a real animal who grows from babyhood to adulthood and has different needs at different stages of development, the same is true of your HMO business.

I've noticed from working with plenty of people over the last few years that there are various stages in an HMO investor's journey that present different challenges and opportunities. Many people want to get to the stage where they are financially free – i.e. where they have enough income coming in from HMOs to pay all their personal bills (mortgage, utilities, car, school fees etc.) but then they're not quite confident enough to grow further so that they can outsource the running of the business to other people. You may have a great managing agent who does the day-to-day activity, but you still have to get involved with some aspects of the tenants and/or maintenance. So, how do you scale up without creating another full-time job? At what point should you outsource and leverage? At what point can you grow and go do something else if you want to?

STAGES OF GROWTH

Stage 1 – is start-up phase where you have 1–3 HMOs and you might still be in a day job or running another business – and you probably run your portfolio fairly easily yourself. Most of the Finding, Finishing and Filling is down to you. It's likely the Funding is also yours. You don't have any staff and few systems. The business runs smoothly most of the time and, apart from the odd short stress point, you are enjoying building the portfolio. This stage can last up to 18 months to two years depending on how fast you can develop your HMOs. If you can start to raise money from other people, your journey will accelerate. I would suggest at this point that you must get a business mentor to help you focus on what is important *not* urgent, so that you utilise your time and energy wisely to get to **Stage 2**.

At Stage 2–you have 4–6 HMOs and you are probably stuck in the 'self-employed landlord' category where you don't feel that you can sustainably outsource enough and still make a profit. You are spending half your time managing your portfolio and finding the competing demands fairly heavy. The benefit is that your profit should be growing nicely and your initial HMOs should be settling down (they often take up to a year to get through teething problems). You will have left your day job (or reduced your hours) and may have become part-time in any other business you are running to concentrate on growing your portfolio. You may have a team of trusted trades who will step in and help you, and you are in charge of coordinating this work. This stage feels like you are growing quite fast and you are able to juggle new projects with the ones already completed. This is a fantastic stage to get to, as it is the key to financial freedom that you have desired for so long. You will have implemented the processes in this book and followed the Five-Step System to resounding success!

Once you get to **Stage 3** (over six HMOs or about 30 or more rooms), you will now be facing the challenge of working full-time in the business *plus* taking on staff, and upscaling your systems through Future-Proofing, so that you can regain your freedom (that you had in stage 1 but have lost in stage 2). At this stage you may be focused internally on your business operations rather than on acquisitions. This is to be expected. You have a large portfolio and you are directing all processes and managing financial transactions on a daily basis.

You now need to use other people's time, and you have the profit to pay others, but the focus should be on ensuring your systems and processes are up to speed and scalable. You may consider diversification and using other strategies. If you are using an agent, you may start to wonder whether you could do a better job by bringing it all 'in-house' but the fear of taking on the role makes you concerned that stepping back in will create another full-time job.

When I was at this stage, I was also running a household with three boys (my eldest had left home by then) and the youngest was seven years old. So, my time was also taken up with homework, football, swimming and playing (the best bit!). I was pretty exhausted much of the time and wondered why we ever bought a TV as I never watched it. My husband had just left his job to join me in the business and everything felt rather chaotic. It is what Roger James Hamilton calls the 'The Octopus Effect'. On the surface, it looks like you or your business is successful because you have money coming in and so much going on; 'beneath the surface, there are many tentacles relying on one small brain, and everything sucks'.

This is often where the turning point comes for many investors – where the size of the portfolio requires great systems run and managed well, to free up the time of the owner. Suddenly, just working harder is not cutting it – and in fact it's leading to more problems. If you are using an outsourced team such as a management agent, there are systems that will be needed to manage the agent. Ultimately the end goal may be to retain the portfolio to pass on to your children and future generations, but systemising your business creates an asset that is also able to be packaged and sold at a price. This is the added value that you (through systems) can bring to your business. It is at this point when you might pause your acquisitions in order to stabilise your business. This is a time when Future-Proofing comes sharply into focus, if it hasn't already.

By **Stage 4** (over 12 HMOs – over 60 units) you will have regained your time from the day-to-day management of the properties and tenants, but now you have systems and staff to manage. Your focus at Stage 3 was to use other people's time, and this alone will have taken a few months to establish. By

Stage 4 your time working *in* the business will have pivoted to being *on* the business. Instilling good routines and rhythms will be essential.

Regular financial, property and staff reviews are required so that you can direct operations without having to run them personally. If you are using a managing agent, the transition to this stage should be fairly smooth as many of the jobs are already being taken care of by the agent. Knowing your monthly profit and loss, and reviewing your cashflow is critical, so a company bookkeeper or accountant is crucial. At this stage measuring the time you spend *on* the business can become one of your key performance indicators. Aim to reduce this by 10% per month until you can confidently say you are balancing responsibility for running a sound business with the resources with which to do it. Once you reach this stage you are in a stronger position to develop a new strategy and expand once more. You will know your business inside out and others will be coming to you for advice and guidance. You may wish to do larger projects, new developments or conversions. This is the stage where that can happen as your HMO business has strong foundations and a structure for stability and steady growth.

Whichever stage you are at now, recognise where you are and what steps you need to take to get to the next stage. It is for this reason that I advise anyone who is investing in HMOs to ensure that they fully apply the Five-Step System per HMO, thus creating a residual income from a handful of properties. If one step is missed, then it's likely that you will continually be Finishing or Future-Proofing or Funding a previous project as you take on a new one. Whilst it can expedite your growth, the risk is that you are left with many aspects of each project incomplete.

I like the phrase 'set, let and forget'. This has been my mantra throughout the time that I have been building my portfolio and has helped me reduce my time exponentially whilst still growing the business. In reality, what seems to happen is that there are huge peaks and troughs where your time is literally eaten up and then spat out. You are stretched beyond measure and then suddenly you regain oodles of time.

Having enough property and income to afford staff and outsourced services allows you the benefit of income and time and only you can decide how many HMOs and rooms will do that for you. Then you can run your portfolio for a few hours per week, still make great money, and do what you love, *or* make a conscious decision to stay in the stage you are at, but borrow learning from the next stage to ease your current pain. Running a successful HMO business will demand some time from you each month. You should aim to reduce this by 10% per month by focusing on staff and systems. Your role is to work **on** and not **in** your business.

BRANDING AND POSITIONING

One area that many investors fail to appreciate is that the portfolio itself has value as a job lot – particularly if you have created a business that can demonstrate sound capital investment, wise gearing and excellent financial management. The element that will take your business from the normal to the super level is its brand. I've come to realise that the best HMO investors don't just focus on the product, the property or the systems. They also develop their brand. Whether you have one or 51 HMOs doesn't matter – it's never too early to think about your brand and your position in the marketplace. It's the one differentiation that will help people choose you over others and creates greater clarity about what you stand for.

'A brand is the set of expectations, memories, stories and relationships that, taken together, account for a consumer's decision to choose one product or service over another'
—Seth Godin

Think of a brand that you use regularly. Whether it's a special brand of shampoo, or a particular soft drink, you choose that brand because of its specific qualities, taste or results. Who doesn't want hair that is super smooth and looks shiny all day? Why choose another brand of soft drink when the one you know and love has a great taste and makes you feel satisfied? That brand represents certain sensory and values-based features. Your interaction with the product or service has a sensory appeal in some way. It tastes, feels or sounds good. It makes you feel a certain way when you consume it. It makes you feel better, stronger, full. This is the power of a good product that is backed by a powerful brand. You too can create a brand that conveys its values and sensory qualities to its consumer in your HMOs. Those businesses (even ones with five properties or less) that create a brand that reflects their values are much more likely to send a clear message to their customers, and attract exactly the right kind of tenant and staff. This is true of any advanced market, such as the HMO market we are in right now.

This is a time when simply having a handful of properties will not be enough to set you apart from the competition and let your rooms shine above the rest. You need to consider what your core reasons are as to why a tenant would want to rent from you and make those messages explicit in your branding and marketing.

My business partner and I struggled to come up with a name that wasn't just 'Wendy and Mark's HMOs Company' when we started to invest together. Accurate, but boring. We went through a few iterations of names before we came up with Best Nest™. It was a memorable moment. I was at home watching TV and Mark was at his home with a glass of port in his hand, when a text came through to me from him: What should we call our business? We exchanged a few messages about wanting to be the best, and also creating a home for tenants where they could fly the nest of their previous home and make their resting place with us. A few more text messages later, and we'd decided on it – Best Nest™. We had a logo designed and trademarked it for posterity.

Does your name really matter? Many of the brands around us have names we accept without question even though they may be rather random choices on the part of the owner. I don't think the name ultimately makes too much of a difference. However, branding *does* make a difference. How you position yourself, frame your messages and create a buzz around your rooms is the result of having a well-thought-out and effective brand.

For us, Best Nest™ was all about quality rooms at a reasonable price. Our tagline when we started was 'Just like a hotel, only it's home'. We soon discovered that tenants expected room service, a concierge and hotel-style laundry facilities. We had a rethink and realised that a better tagline would be 'Best Rooms,

Best Prices, Best Nest'. It conveyed more honestly and realistically what we delivered. Simple, yet effective. If you can come up with a simple tagline to your business and demonstrate alignment with that in what you do, you have the makings of a great brand. You may be small to start with, and your plan might be to create five HMOs making £1,000 profit per month. This doesn't mean that you shouldn't put some creative muscle into making your properties stand out from the crowd – and branding is a core part of that approach.

Your customers are tenants, and the initial contact a customer (or potential tenant) has with your brand will be a sensory one. They will *see* or *read* about your rooms or houses on your website, Facebook page and other advertising portals. Your brand is conveyed initially through the senses. Have you ever asked potential tenants how they have felt after coming across your written material/advertising copy or adverts? The way that you use colour, shape, form and typography in your logo is just the beginning. If you're not sure about how to design an effective logo (and there are plenty of free logo-making web applications available), commission a designer to create one for you. www.99designs.com specialises in logo design. People per hour, Upwork and Fiverr are also very useful sites for commissioning graphic design.

As well as the visual appearance of your company brand, the interface with your HMO is equally important to understanding your brand and conveying it well. They will *feel* and *touch* the actual walls and carpets, flooring, kitchens that you have installed when they do a viewing. If they are desperate, you may even allow them to experience the toilet facilities on a viewing (yes this has happened to me!) Have you ever asked tenants how they felt after a viewing – not just emotionally, but the sensory aspects such as smell, sight and touch. These aspects are rarely made plain or obvious. However, they have a direct impact on how your customers will feel emotionally – and we know that buying is usually as much an emotional as a logical process.

In property, this could be rooms that are beautifully lit, have good space for personal belongings, have other tenants who share the same lifestyle or have clean and well-maintained bathroom facilities. How you present your rooms, how you communicate your unique selling points (USPs) and how you manage and maintain your properties contributes to your brand.

Some questions for reflection:

- How can I work with my agent to help communicate my unique brand?
- How do I want my tenants to feel once they've done a viewing at one of my properties?
- How can I make that happen?
- What do I believe are the unique selling points of my brand?
- How can I demonstrate that in the way I run my business?
- Who do I need to impress upon my values and my brand?
- How can I ensure consistency and reliability within the messages I present?

As your business matures and develops, you'll learn exponentially about what makes property work. From a handful of ordinary properties, your experiences of actually doing it will teach you far more than you ever realised was possible. By implementing the Five-Step System detailed in this book, you will not only learn the basics about investing, but also some fairly advanced strategies. Your learning should not end there. You need to ensure that you are scaling your own growth by networking, advancing your education and developing your investing mindset. Your own growth is central to the growth of your business. Whether you want to own five or 500 properties is up to you: your scale will depend wholly on your ability to manage the associated growing pains and to determine your own level of success.

CHAPTER 12
THE FUTURE OF HMOS

'The future depends on what we do in the present'
—Mahatma Gandhi

If you're excited about the prospects of what HMOs can do for you, I'm with you. I truly believe they remain a life-changing strategy for many people. You only need a handful to make job-equivalent income and, when systemised properly, they can be a way to completely transform your life. Over the last few years, the attraction of high returns that are offered by HMOs, paired with the ability to advertise rooms more conveniently through the internet, has meant that far more investors are keen to develop HMOs. Apart from specific actions that investors can take to choose the area wisely, to future-proof their property and work with a proactive agent, what can we learn from current market conditions that might affect HMO supply? Where will this lead? Are there better opportunities for investors or do HMOs still have a place in a profitable portfolio? If you are someone considering investing and would like to know more about the potential future of HMOs, then in this section I aim to give you an overview of where we are currently in terms of the UK landscape.

HOUSING SUPPLY

Housing has always been a political football. Since the end of the Second World War, when the UK government recognised the need for extensive development in residential property to house soldiers and their families back from the war, there has been a constant drive to build new homes. As mentioned earlier, varying governments of different political persuasions have sought to address annual shortfalls in new builds and, apart from a couple of instances, failed miserably to hit their targets.

Since the 1970s, building enough houses for the population has been a constant battle for successive UK governments. The complexity of planning regulations, local policies, land prices and builder/developer interests has led to many stagnant years of house building. In 2018 alone it was estimated that the UK would need to build an additional 250,000 houses per annum (social and regular houses). To illustrate the enormity of the figure, it means a house being built every 10 minutes for every day of the year.

New legislation is constantly being passed to encourage new house building in the UK, yet the volume of houses needed is so great that it will take years to create as many homes as are needed. Ironically there are many houses in a state of abandonment or disrepair, which local councils have a duty to deal with. The intricacies of dealing with absent home owners or landlords means that many of these properties languish interminably on residential streets, creating an eyesore and reducing by one more the number of residential properties available. Although needing repair, upgrade and renovation, these properties could be sold at auction or the owners given incentives to sell or renovate. These are often ideal for development into HMOs. First-time and family buyers don't usually have the knowledge or inclination to buy a run-down property and spend time and money on renovations. This is where investors are helping the local economy: buying property that otherwise would be standing empty and renovating them for the purposes of providing additional housing.

It is easy to look at the apparent lack of availability of property as being the reason why young people and couples cannot buy property. The truth is that they cannot get lending to buy a suitable property. It is well known that the money supply has a far greater influence on the housing market than availability of property. It influences house prices, confidence in the market, builder and developer commitment and buyer confidence. Although we might like to think that buying a house is a marker of social status, historically the UK has been a country where many people have never owned their own property.

With the lack of supply fuelling higher demand, and the reduction of eligibility to mortgages for many people, renting is their sole solution. HMOs offer a certain step on that rental ladder for many people – especially those straight out of university or coming to the UK for work. Housing supply in the build-to-rent sector is gathering pace, but currently the focus is on cities rather than larger towns: places where traditional HMOs work beautifully well. There is no doubt that the catch-up needed to supply homes for individuals and families will take many years to accomplish and, in that time, the UK is facing a bottle neck. Landlords and investor are actively needed to plug the gap. Despite the government's uplift of structural barriers to local landlords (tax changes and increasing legal demands such as

HMO licensing), I fail to see how many people would live, were there not an active PRS. HMOs are a core part of that sector and, in my mind, create huge solutions for the government in supplying a much needed rental housing supply.

FUTURE OF THE PRS AND HMOS

As HMOs have become more mainstream in the minds of investors, the media and the government, they have attracted more attention and interest. In conjunction with their establishment as a sustainable and dependable form of housing, there has been a growing backlash against landlords and those using property investment to grow their wealth. Aimed not just at HMO landlords, but anyone who owns property in addition to their own home, the UK government has introduced a raft of legislation to reduce income and profits for investors. The latest tax changes aside, we're seeing changes introduced that make renting property much less attractive and sustainable: the imposition of fees on tenancy set-ups; the abolition of section 21 (tenant no-fault eviction); the discourse about rent controls and the right to buy.

The notion of home ownership is rapidly changing and many people accept that being a home owner is not necessarily a status symbol they aspire to. The flexibility of renting, coupled with relatively low entry fees means that for many people renting is their only option. They exercise a choice to rent. The problem comes when someone (often a couple) want to buy but don't have enough money for the deposit or cannot get a mortgage of sufficient size for the property they would like to buy.

Will we see HMOs in the style of co-living retirement homes, which cater solely for those who in their retirement have nowhere to live? Perhaps HMOs will use pension credits to provide for older people. With social housing at a stretch already, and the social care budget creaking and an ageing population, you might need to install a stair lift in your next refurb!

BANK LENDING AND MORTGAGE REGULATIONS

Following the banking credit crunch and ensuing market crash in 2007–2008, banking lending regulation has increased massively. This means that while banks and lenders may want to lend money (and indeed for the growth of their business they *need to*), the regulatory framework in which they operate is tightly restricted to those who meet their fairly stringent requirements. This has led to much tighter acceptance criteria. This means that customers who want to borrow for mortgage purposes are often continually locked out of the opportunity to buy.

According to the Council of Mortgage Lenders, 1.7 million buy-to-let loans have been advanced since the market started to be monitored in 1999. Over this time, the private rented sector has doubled in size, following decades of steady decline. Indeed, outstanding buy-to-let mortgage balances recently grew to more than £200 billion – equivalent to the gross domestic product of Hong Kong. The recovery has seen annual buy-to-let lending expand to £27 billion last year from a low point of £9 billion in 2009. It is currently running at an annual rate of about £33 billion. Data from the Council of Mortgage Lenders (September 2015) shows that the buy-to-let sector has been the predominant recovery story in the mortgage market since the financial crisis of 2007.In absolute terms, however, buy-to-let lending for both house purchase and remortgaging are still some way short of their peak levels in 2007. Other data from the CML shows that:

- Buy-to-let has grown from around 9% of all lending for house purchase in 2010 to account for 14% of this activity today. However, buy-to-let accounted for 17% of house purchase lending in 2007.
- Arrears on buy-to-let loans have been falling since 2009, reflecting the pattern of arrears across the mortgage market as a whole. But the decline in buy-to-let arrears has been more pronounced than in the wider market, so that the rate is now below its equivalent in the owner-occupied sector.
- The strong growth of buy-to-let and recovery of the private rented sector, have been supported by a range of factors, including increasing numbers of young people in higher education, large inward net migration, reduced job security and availability of social housing, tightening affordability pressures on would-be owner-occupiers and poor returns on pensions and investments. Within the lending sector, there has also been improved credit availability and increased competition between firms.
- There are currently around 1,100 buy-to-let mortgage products, the highest number since April 2008.[14]

In January 2017 the Prudential Regulation Authority – part of the Bank of England – told lenders to become much stricter about their policies around buy-to-let mortgages. This led to an increase in the amount of rent that lenders wanted to see, in order to cover monthly mortgage payments, to145%. It also

14 Council of Mortgage Lenders, 2017.

imposed a new 'stress test', requiring landlords to be able to show they would be able to afford to cover the mortgage if interest rates went up to 5.5% over five years. These changes fell beautifully into the lap of HMOs where it is not hard to create cashflow of at least £1,000 per month, which is well over the 145% required income to cover mortgage interest level requirement. HMO mortgages are usually classified as commercial lending, which falls outside of the FCA regulations. They offer more flexibility and opportunity to build a portfolio.

NB: Always seek professional advice when getting a mortgage for an HMO. New products from lenders are constantly entering the market, and your particular situation will govern the type of mortgage you are entitled to.

SERVICED ACCOMMODATION (SA)

The strategy known as serviced accommodation (think Airbnb if you are struggling to conceptualise it) has grown as a contrasting investment strategy over the last few years. The beauty of SA is that it complements HMOs, except it is aimed at short-term and holiday type lets rather than longer-term rental accommodation. The refurb and set-up process is very similar to an HMO and, depending on the area of the country in which you are investing, SA might prove to be a lucrative bolt-on strategy to your HMO strategy.

There are downsides to SA that HMOs don't incur, such as management of cleaners, laundry and 'services'. Ensuring your units (rooms or property) are full and achieving maximum occupancy will require you to set up accounts with Booking.com and

Airbnb as a bare minimum. You will need to have a channel manager (an online system that coordinates bookings between sites to ensure you don't have double bookings) and most likely you'll need a member of staff to dedicate a certain portion of time per week to manage it. Most SA operators agree that the business is far from hands-free. However, there can be excellent returns achieved by SA and the tax treatment is more favourable as these are counted as holiday lettings, not income from residential property. If you can organise your business so that a member of staff manages the operations for you, you can certainly make significant profits. SA will not work in all areas of the country and you may find that the costs of operating are only offset when you have a certain number of units so that you can gain economies of scale.

Limitations to lengths of stay by guests are being imposed on operators in cities like London to ensure that SA does not subsume residential accommodation availability.

CO-LIVING

Co-living has become a by-word for communal shared HMO living that is more personal and cooperative than a traditional HMO. Spaces may be delineated for working and playing as well as living, and amenities may include additions such as TV room with widescreen cinema-style media, and larger kitchen diner space.

Across the world where space for living individually is tight, co-living has been the norm, especially in communities where people have shared interests and a common purpose, such as religious communities. Reflecting these more esoteric groups who share meals and activities to create a more sustainable and possibly ecologically friendly way of life, these communities have influenced HMO co-living. Unlike international co-living communities, these are a somewhat stripped-down version: there is less age spread of tenants yet a more idealistic way of community living is attempted. Time will tell how successful this brand of HMO becomes. It may be a fad or it may be a trend that enables HMO tenants to feel a sense of belonging and community, that is often missing in a room-by-room HMO.

BREXIT

Another political hot potato which at the time of writing is still not resolved, despite three years passing since the public referendum. Whatever shape our eventual relationship is with Europe will inevitably cast a cloud on some part of the economy. Which part that is remains to be seen. There are risks in staying in and risks in leaving. Aside from Brexit, the patterns of economic activity that we as investors should be aware of are immigration, bank lending policy, interest and inflation rates and national productivity. These areas can all be examined in the light of our relationship with the EU – whatever form that takes.

Where does this leave the HMO investor? As Heraclitus (the Greek philosopher) said 'Constant change is here to stay'. As investors we are looking for the best solution for long-term wealth and income. We have to stay abreast of changes and not allow cynicism or disappointment to cloud our judgement.

THE TIME IS NOW

In an advanced marketplace where there is competition from many sectors, the HMO market continues to grow and thrive. Landlords who set up business years ago have seen huge changes and the UK government has introduced legislation that has undoubtedly put a squeeze on the income of HMO owners. For some, this has led to apathy and disillusionment about HMOs as a source of residual income. There is no doubt that the current climate is a testing one for investors, but there are advantages too. Many people will not evolve their approach quickly enough to embrace the principles and practice of a profitable, twenty-first century HMO business. They will deem it to be too hard or too challenging. They will resist finding the right property and they won't invest enough to make good quality rooms that will easily rent. They will look for licensing short-cuts and short-term gains and then declare 'it can't be done'. HMOs, though, are not a 'get rich quick' strategy. You can make extraordinary profits from ordinary properties, but not if you don't educate yourself and take action.

In order to create a profitable, systematised HMO business that runs with very little of your time, you will have to accept that this is not a hobby. It is a business to be taken seriously, studied and learnt; then you will create income for a lifestyle and wealth for a legacy. The facts and opinions listed above are to encourage you to engage in the discourse around property investing and to help educate you as to why now is a great time to make money from property. I believe in HMOs as a fast and effective way to create income, to free up your time from a job, and to change your life through investing in assets.

You are benefiting yourself, your family and your customers (tenants) by getting involved in this exciting and profitable aspect of property. The time is right now to be doing this. We have not seen a more competitive edge when more and more people are looking for rooms to rent, and when the opportunity for the savvy investor is so obviously present. Interest rates are at an all-time low and many factors in the economy point to a steady and growing need for all-inclusive room rents. As one of my mentors once said 'Don't wait to invest in property. Invest in property and wait.'

Having invested in property for over 20 years, I have the benefit of hindsight and insight (sadly not foresight or I would be buying my National Lottery ticket today). My experience teaches me that weathering the changes is as much a skill of the investor as spotting the trends, the new waves, the events coming over the horizon. In my view, the outlook for HMOs is very good if you get it right from the start. It might end up being a strategy that we all come to accept as a necessity to enable the growth of our country.

You only need a handful to make a difference to your life. If you follow the steps in this book, you too can make extraordinary profits from ordinary properties and, as a result, have the freedom to make choices for your and your family's future. Step up, make the decision to say yes and get going. Don't let fear hold you back as you strive to create an extraordinary life of your own.

CHAPTER 13

YOUR FUTURE, YOUR DREAMS

'The future belongs to those who believe in the beauty of their dreams'
—Eleanor Roosevelt

You may have picked up this book because you wanted to understand in depth how to create extraordinary profits from ordinary property. Or you may have a dream that has lain dormant and for which you need extra income. Or perhaps it was the lure of high cashflow coupled with freedom that attracts you. Possibly it was all three. I am a fan of HMOs for the freedom, lifestyle and income that they bring. More importantly perhaps because getting on the HMO train will take you places you never expected to be.

Most people start investing in property for two reasons: cashflow and capital appreciation. If you get a good mixture of both, you'll do well. The perfect mixture of revenue and capital provides an excellent compound effect for the future and income for now. You will find that in years to come you have a profitable and highly valuable portfolio, giving you many options. HMOs are no exception – being the one asset class that can be highly leveraged, allowing you fast cashflow. You can build substantial extra income streams from a handful of houses. Once you have a handful of ordinary properties creating extraordinary profits, you will face some decisions. Should you continue to grow the portfolio in the same way, as in a cookie-cutter approach? Should you diversify into other strategies? Should you take the money and retire?

This all depends on whether you want to focus more on lifestyle or legacy. You can, of course, do both. The wonderful part of property investing is that once it is properly set up, let out and systemised, you will have choices about your life and what you can do with your time. What are the dreams that you've shelved as the 9–5 has ebbed away your energies? Which destinations across the world appeal to you to venture forth and explore? How would you love to spend your time? Are there other business ideas you're itching to get going with? Consider the feeling of not having to swap your time for money any longer – and instead have the time and income to pursue your passions. This truly is freedom!

You know now my simple Five-Step System:

1. Find it
2. Fund It
3. Finish It
4. Fill It
5. Future-Proof It

Follow these steps and you can create an amazing portfolio with just five ordinary properties that bring extraordinary profits for the rest of your life.

ACTION STATION

What are your top five reasons for investing in HMOs?

1.
2.
3.
4.
5.

What is your financial freedom figure?

When is the deadline for achieving your financial freedom figure?

How will you celebrate when you have five cashflowing HMOs?

What is holding you back from starting today?

What action steps do you need to take now?

This chapter is about *you* – your aspirations, your desires, your dreams. The plans you made when you were ten years old to be rich and famous, to excel at sport, to fly to the moon. The dreams you once had to travel, explore, be present. The people and causes that are important to you but for whom you've had no time. Perhaps the feeling that you *could* leave your job if you wanted to – thus making it less of a chore and more of a calling.

Once you've created residual income the world is your oyster – now go and find the pearl that is your life.

ABOUT THE AUTHOR

Wendy Whittaker-Large is the founder of multiple companies including Best Nest – a high-end HMO company – and Best Nest Egg (an HMO investment club). Over the last 20 years she has steadily built a multi-million pound property portfolio whilst raising a family and running an award-winning training business. She is passionate about HMOs for their contribution to the housing economy and the positive impact they can make to people's lives. She is a published author and her book *101 Essential Tips for Running a Professional HMO* is an Amazon bestseller. She has been featured in the *Sunday Telegraph* and regularly appears on the property speaking circuit. She was also a finalist in the Landlord and Letting Awards 2016. Wendy now helps other people to achieve financial freedom whilst juggling business and family commitments through investing in HMOs.

https://www.wendywl.uk
https://twitter.com/TheHMOqueen
https://www.facebook.com/wendywlarge
https://facebook.com/groups/TheUltimateHMOSuccessSystem
https://www.youtube.com/user/wendywl

101 Essential Tips
for RUNNING A PROFESSIONAL HMO
giving you time, money and freedom
by Wendy Whittaker-Large
101 Essential Tips for RUNNING A PROFESSIONAL HMO WENDY WHITTAKER-LARGE

ALSO BY

WENDY WHITTAKER-LARGE

'101 Essential Tips for Running a Professional HMO – Giving you Time, Money and Freedom'

Across the UK more and more people are choosing to live in Houses of Multiple Occupation and, as the market grows, so do the demands of the tenants. If you are considering entering this market and wish to find out how to develop an HMO that it is profitable, well managed and well maintained, then this book is for you. All tips have been implemented, tested and refined through repeated processes and will help you to create a systemised business that will successfully run itself. This book is a handy guide to help you quickly and efficiently learn some tricks of the trade and apply them in your chosen HMO location. Using the knowledge in this book you will be able to create a systemised business that runs even when you're not there. This book is focused on the professional HMO market, but many of the tips can easily be applied to other sectors of the market such as LHA (local housing allowance) and student HMOs.